# 50

# QUALITY IMPROVEMENT & QUALITY ASSURANCE APPROACHES

Sara Miller McCune founded SAGE Publishing in 1965 to support the dissemination of usable knowledge and educate a global community. SAGE publishes more than 1000 journals and over 800 new books each year, spanning a wide range of subject areas. Our growing selection of library products includes archives, data, case studies and video. SAGE remains majority owned by our founder and after her lifetime will become owned by a charitable trust that secures the company's continued independence.

Los Angeles | London | New Delhi | Singapore | Washington DC | Melbourne

# 50

# QUALITY IMPROVEMENT & QUALITY ASSURANCE APPROACHES

Simple, easy and effective
ways to improve performance

## SHARRON MANSELL

EDITOR

## ANN GRAVELLS

WITH ILLUSTRATIONS BY

ANDREW HAMPEL

LM Learning Matters

A SAGE Publishing Company

Learning Matters
A SAGE Publishing Company
1 Oliver's Yard
55 City Road
London EC1Y 1SP

SAGE Publications Inc.
2455 Teller Road
Thousand Oaks, California 91320

SAGE Publications India Pvt Ltd
B 1/I 1 Mohan Cooperative Industrial Area
Mathura Road
New Delhi 110 044

SAGE Publications Asia-Pacific Pte Ltd
3 Church Street
#10-04 Samsung Hub
Singapore 049483

Editor: Amy Thornton
Senior project editor: Chris Marke
Project management: Deer Park Productions
Marketing manager: Dilhara Attygalle
Cover design: Wendy Scott
Typeset by: C&M Digitals (P) Ltd, Chennai, India
Printed in the UK

**Library of Congress Control Number: 2020945715**

**British Library Cataloguing in Publication Data**

A catalogue record for this book is available from the
British Library

ISBN 978-1-5297-2694-7
ISBN 978-1-5297-2693-0 (pbk)

At SAGE we take sustainability seriously. Most of our products are printed in the UK using responsibly sourced
papers and boards. When we print overseas we ensure sustainable papers are used as measured by the
Egmont grading system. We undertake an annual audit to monitor our sustainability.

# Contents

## Appendices

# Acknowledgements

I would like to give a special thanks to the following people who have helped me with the production of this book. They have freely given their time, knowledge and advice, which has resulted in some excellent contributions and additions to the content. Without their amazing proofreading skills and honest feedback, this book would not be what it is, and I am truly grateful.

Adrienne Pye – External Quality Assurer at VTCT

Emma Woodhall – Head of Centre at White Rose Beauty Colleges Sheffield

Debbie Forsythe-Conroy – Education Consultant and External inspector

Lisa Morris – Director at Educating UK & Lead External Quality Assurer at TQUK

Louise C Gulbrandsen – QTS Med, Teacher at Loavenstad School

Michael Sinanis – Assistant Principal Corporate Services at White Rose Beauty Colleges

Nina Reed – Head of Centre & Lead Internal Quality Assurer at White Rose Beauty Colleges Manchester

Shelley Gledhill – Independent End Point Assessor at City and Guilds

I would like to express a special thank you to my boss, Karen Lee-Cooke, Principal of the White Rose Beauty Colleges, for her words of encouragement and the trust and opportunities she has given me.

I would like to thank Richard, Emma, Steven and Morgan for their continued support and patience.

I would also like to thank my Senior Commissioning Editor (Education) Amy Thornton for her support and guidance.

This book would not have happened without the help and support of my editor Ann Gravells who has patiently detangled my dyslexic language and writing, and given me so much more confidence in my own ability. Ann's calm, organised and professional approach to life is truly inspirational. Also, my illustrator Andrew Hampel who never fails to amaze me with his creative ideas for each chapter title. So huge thanks to them.

Every effort has been made to trace the copyright holders and to obtain their permission for the use of copyright material. The publisher, editor and author will gladly receive any information enabling them to rectify any error or omission in subsequent editions.

Sharron Mansell

# Author statement

## Sharron Mansell

Sharron started delivering education and training programmes on a part-time basis in 1987, before progressing into a full-time career in further education in 2000. She has gained practical work-based skills and a wide and varied under-standing of schools' provision, further and higher education, apprenticeships and full-cost courses.

Starting her career as a teacher in a land-based specialist college, she progressed to course management before taking responsibility for several departments. Sharron further developed her knowledge and skills within the sector when her role changed to Head of Services to Business and ESOL within a large further education college. She is currently the Deputy Principal at the White Rose Beauty Colleges, and their Ofsted nominee. It is recognised as the UK's largest beauty therapy training provider which was judged *outstanding* by Ofsted in 2019.

Sharron is passionate about raising standards in education, and is committed to supporting quality improvement at all levels and stages. She also works part-time as an external inspector and is on the board of governors for a local primary school.

Sharron holds an Honour's Degree in Education and Training, a Certificate in Education, is a Member of the Society for Education and Training, and holds QTLS status.

**She is the author of:**

*50 Teaching and Learning Approaches*

*50 Assessment Approaches*

*Achieving QTLS Status*

**Sharron can be contacted via:**

Facebook: https://www.facebook.com/mansellsharron/

Twitter: https://twitter.com/sharronmansell

LinkedIn: https://www.linkedin.com/in/sharronmansell

Email: sharronmansell@outlook.com

# Editor statement

**Ann Gravells**

Ann has been teaching, assessing and quality assuring in the further education and training sector since 1983. She is a director of her own company *Ann Gravells Ltd*, an educational consultancy based in East Yorkshire. She specialises in teaching, training, assessment and quality assurance.

Ann holds a Master's in Educational Management, a PGCE, a Degree in Education, and a City & Guilds Medal of Excellence for teaching. She is a Fellow of the Society for Education and Training, and holds QTLS status.

Ann has been writing and editing textbooks since 2006, which are mainly based on her own experiences as a teacher and the subsequent education of trainee teachers. She aims to write in plain English to help anyone with their role. She creates resources for teachers and learners such as PowerPoints, online courses and handouts for the assessment, quality assurance, and teacher training qualifications. These are available via her website: www.anngravells.com

Ann has worked for several awarding organisations producing qualification guidance, policies and procedures, and carrying out the external quality assurance of teaching, assessment and quality assurance qualifications.

She is an Ofqual Assessment Specialist, a consultant to The University of Cambridge's Institute of Continuing Education, and a technical advisor to the awarding organisation Training Qualifications UK (TQUK).

Ann Gravells
www.anngravells.com

# Illustrator statement

**Andrew Hampel**

Andrew is a designer and lecturer who has been delivering and managing further and higher education art and design courses since 2000. His design work ranges from traditional watercolour to multimedia video performance pieces.

Outside education, Andrew is a partner in an event company *District 14*, providing marketing and corporate presentations for comic cons.

Having a direct link to the vocational design industry gives his students an excellent opportunity to work directly with his company to provide workshops and materials to the community, along with access to a wide range of professionals including Marvel and BBC Books.

As well as design work, Andrew has a passion for history and is a trustee for a World War Two home front project. He has a special responsibility for educational projects and community outreach.

Andrew has contributed writing to a number of science fiction anthology works and podcasts, as well as writing and illustrating *Quick Histories of Hull*.

Andrew's Online Folio can be seen at: deviantart.com/skaromedia

Andrew can be contacted via email: skaromedia@hotmail.com

# Foreword

If you are looking for innovative, yet easy and effective ways to perform your quality role, then the chapters in this book are just what you need.

Whether you are new to quality or are experienced, the approaches in this book will give you lots of ideas to put theory into practice. They might help you to try something different or to adapt what you currently do.

Just like Sharron's other books – *50 Teaching and Learning Approaches* and *50 Assessment Approaches* – I wished a book like these had been available when I first started my role as a quality manager, and as an internal (IQA) and external quality assurer (EQA). It's fine to read textbooks all about the theory regarding quality, but it's putting it into practice that matters, which this book will help to do.

Sharron has included a few traditional quality approaches such *creating and updating policies and procedures, standardising practice* and *making decisions when sampling evidence,* and added lots of other exciting approaches such as *managing risks and contingency planning, preparing for an external inspection* and *undertaking joint work scrutiny.*

Do try out some or all of the approaches, and feel free to adjust them to suit your subject, your team members and assessors, and the environment within which the approach will take place. Some aspects referred to in the book might change over time, for example; Ofsted often update their inspection framework, so always check for the latest version.

You will find three completed examples of records in the appendices. Appendix 1 will prove useful if you are new to creating an IQA sample plan and tracking sheet. Appendix 2 is a completed example of a standardisation record for assessed work, and Appendix 3 is a work plan for a lead internal quality assurer.

Both Sharron and I hope you enjoy the book. Please feel free to give us some feedback here: http://www.anngravells.com/anns-books/book-reviews

Other books in the series:

*50 Teaching and Learning Approaches*
*50 Assessment Approaches*

Ann Gravells
www.anngravells.com

# Introduction

## Your role

Whether your role relates to quality improvement or quality assurance, your main purpose is to ensure your organisation at least meets the requirements of the areas you are responsible for. This might include (in alphabetical order):

- creating and implementing policies, procedures and other documentation
- evaluating and monitoring products and/or services
- identifying and mitigating risks
- interpreting and implementing legislative, regulatory and mandatory requirements
- leading on teaching, learning and assessment activities
- making decisions
- managing and training staff and teams
- managing budgets
- managing resources
- reviewing and updating processes and practices
- standardising practice
- supporting and managing learners and other stakeholders.

Undertaking a role in quality improvement or quality assurance requires you to have or to develop exceptional communication and organisational skills, adaptability and flexibility, and be attuned to your environment and the people around you. You will need to have confidence in your own abilities and be inspirational to the people you work with. In addition, you will need to demonstrate integrity and professionalism in everything you do.

## Using this book

This book is not about theory, it's about giving you some ideas for quality improvement and quality assurance activities which you can try out. It is aimed at settings of all ages from primary school through colleges and private training organisations, to universities.

Throughout the book you will find traditional approaches that have been recognised as good practice for years as well as some new activities. They may not all work, perhaps due to different settings and the qualifications offered, or you can adapt them to suit your own organisation's requirements

The chapters are set out in alphabetical order and you may choose to read the book from start to finish, or to select a title from the contents page to locate a specific activity.

At the end of the book you will find useful appendices to support some of the chapters:

1. example of a completed IQA sampling plan and tracking sheet

2. example of a completed standardisation record for assessed work

3. example of a completed workplan for a lead internal quality assurer

4. career guidance for schools and colleges

# Chapter grids

Each chapter starts with a grid to indicate how the activities can be used. You can see if they relate to internal or external quality assurance (IQA/EQA) and if it is a deep dive activity (see further into this chapter). It shows if the activity can be carried out in person, remotely or electronically/online, and whether it involves learners, assessors and/or others such as teachers. You can also see at a glance if the activity promotes standardisation, whether it's mainly performed by a lead IQA and/or if it is part of a quality improvement role.

# Chapter structure

Each chapter has a series of headings to help you understand how to use the activities.

*What is it?* – an explanation of what the activity is, how to set it up and where it can be used.

*What can it be used for?* – suggests how best you can use the activity to carry out quality improvement and/or quality assurance measures.

*Resources* – lists materials and equipment that might be required to undertake the activity.

*Advantages* – lists the benefits of using the activity.

*Disadvantages* – lists difficulties or challenges you may find with the activity.

Some of the chapters have specific examples, and at the end of every chapter you will find a handy *tip,* and a short list of references for *further reading and weblinks.*

The chapters are cleverly illustrated with characters who are non-gender specific and reflect inclusivity, equality and diversity.

# What is quality improvement?

Quality improvement is about having systems in place to continuously monitor and improve all aspects within an organisation, not just their products or services. It is reliant on active participation from all staff at all levels.

Over recent years, the focus on quality improvement has become more prominent driven by political and economic factors. Schools, further education and skills providers, and higher education have been given more autonomy than ever before. However, they are accountable for the quality of their provision and how any public money they receive is spent. This has led to changes in regulatory processes and compliance, for example; the way external inspections are undertaken.

Continuous monitoring and evaluating honestly and truthfully all aspects of your organisation's affairs will support you to consistently plan and implement quality improvement activities. This should lead to sustained exceptional outcomes for staff, learners and other stakeholders.

# What is quality assurance?

Quality assurance is about having systems in place to ensure that the assessment process is valid and reliable and has been undertaken with integrity.

If quality assurance does not take place, there could be risks to the accuracy, consistency and fairness of training and assessment practice. Quality assurance should be a continual process with the aim of maintaining and improving the products and services offered.

If there is no external formal examination taken by learners, there has to be a system of monitoring the performance of trainers and assessors and the experiences of the learners. If not, assessors might make incorrect judgements or pass a learner who hasn't met the requirements, perhaps because they were biased towards them or they had made a mistake.

# Internal quality assurance

Internal quality assurance (IQA) relates to the monitoring of all the teaching, learning and assessment activities which learners, trainees or employees will undertake. Internal quality assurance is not something that is added on to the end of a qualification or a programme of learning. It should be carried out on an ongoing basis with a view to making improvements, or keeping the status quo if everything is satisfactory. Records must be maintained of all monitoring activities to prove they actually took place, and to facilitate improvements as necessary.

There are other terms used for internal quality assurance which you might come across. For example, internal *verification* and internal *moderation*.

Often, internal quality assurers are also experienced teachers, trainers and assessors in the subject area they are quality assuring. For example, if the subject area is motor vehicle maintenance, they should not be internally quality assuring other subjects they are not experienced in, such as horticulture. The IQA process might be the same for each subject, but the internal quality assurer must be fully familiar with what is being assessed to make a valid and reliable decision. Valid means you are doing what you should, and reliable means you would get similar results each time you did it.

As an internal quality assurer only *samples* various activities, there is the possibility that some aspects might be missed. Imagine this taking place in a bakery, the quality assurer would not sample every item by tasting each one made. They would only taste a sample from each baker, otherwise there would be nothing left to sell. This means there are often risks involved with sampling.

# External quality assurance

External quality assurance (EQA) relates to the monitoring of training, assessment and IQA processes within a centre which has been approved by an awarding organisation (AO) to deliver and assess their qualifications. Any organisation can become an approved centre providing they meet the qualification and the AO's requirements.

External quality assurance must take place on behalf of an awarding organisation to ensure the learners who have been registered with them have received a quality service. It also seeks to ensure that teaching, training, assessment and internal quality assurance have been conducted in a consistent, safe and fair manner.

Learners, when they successfully complete a qualification, will receive a certificate with the awarding organisation's name on, as well as the centre's name. Therefore, the EQA must ensure everything is in order, or the AO's reputation, as well as the centre's, could be brought into disrepute.

# Deep dive

A deep dive is an in-depth look at specific subjects which are delivered by an organisation. Rather than making judgements on a teacher's ability from one observation or from available data, a deep dive enables you to take a more objective and holistic approach.

The methodology of a deep dive is focused on the scrutiny of intent, implementation and impact of the curriculum on learners and other stakeholders. A deep dive uses a range of activities to triangulate and validate findings from the learner journey. For example; a small group of learners could be selected and tracked from the initial advice and guidance they received prior to enrolling on the AO's programme to the point they are at now.

Activities with these learners might include:

- looking at their starting point, their aspirations and targets (does the programme of study support the learners' aspirations?)

- scrutinising the induction process which learners experienced at the start of their programme
- carrying out learning walks
- scrutinising learner work
- looking at teacher feedback and how that feedback has impacted on the learners
- interviewing employers, especially those for apprentices, but could include work experience employers
- interviews with learners which could include the sequencing of learning, why a particular topic is being delivered at a particular stage, and how prior knowledge and skills are being incorporated into delivery
- questioning learners about how they are supported to remember what they have learnt, and how they can relate the learning to everyday life (sometimes known as *sticky learning*)
- looking at any planned progression to higher levels of learning or employment and how this fits with the learner's starting point.

A deep dive should not focus on data, it should follow the evidence, and be objective not subjective.

# Further reading

Belbin M (2010) *Team Roles At Work* (2nd edn). Oxford: Butterworth-Heinemann.

Gravells A (2016) *Principles and Practices of Quality Assurance.* London: Learning Matters.

Inglis J (2014) *Sticky Learning.* Minneapolis: Fortress Press.

Kirkpatrick D & Kirkpatrick J (2006) *Evaluating Training Programs.* Oakland: Berrett-Koehler.

Pleasance S (2016) *Wider Professional Practice in Education and Training.* London: SAGE Publishing.

Read H (2012) *The Best Quality Assurer's Guide.* Bideford: Read On Publications.

Stufflebeam D & Coryn C (2014) *Evaluation Theory, Models and Applications.* San Francisco: Jossey-Bass.

Wood J & Dickinson J (2011) *Quality Assurance and Evaluation in the Lifelong Learning Sector.* Exeter: Learning Matters.

# Weblinks

External quality assurance – https://tinyurl.com/v4at54b

Internal quality assurance and risks – https://tinyurl.com/ybydj7ol

International Organisation for Standardisation (ISO) – https://tinyurl.com/yb5m2e29

Lean process – https://tinyurl.com/y8ojvopt

Self-assessment – https://tinyurl.com/yygsgx7y

Self-evaluation – https://tinyurl.com/k6stxhb

Six stigma – https://tinyurl.com/ycnokagn

# 1 Agreeing action plans

| IQA activity | √ | EQA activity | √ | Deep dive activity | √ |
|---|---|---|---|---|---|
| In person | √ | Remote | √ | Electronic/online | √ |
| Includes learners | √ | Includes assessors | √ | Includes others | √ |
| Promotes standardisation | √ | Lead IQA role | √ | Quality improvement role | √ |

## What is it?

An action plan is a concise document agreed with an individual, team or organisation in relation to their requirements and needs. This is to improve, implement or maintain something, and to support performance. The plan states what specific tasks need to be undertaken, how they will be carried out and by when, and the measures for success.

Depending on what the action plan is being used for, it may include requirements relating to regulations or standards which must be met to offer a particular qualification, or to support an individual to meet the requirements of their job role. It may also include actions relating to improvement or development points to further enhance performance. Equally it may refer to best practice and how this can be shared.

Action plans should include specific, measurable, achievable, realistic and time bound (SMART) targets. They should be revisited on a regular basis and updated with the progress which has been made.

## What can it be used for?

An action plan is used to achieve a specific goal, target, aim or objective.

Action plans can cover a range of activities including:

- as part of the appraisal process or if there is a performance or development requirement. For example, a member of staff may need to update their industry experience to continue delivering and assessing a qualification. An action plan for continuing professional development (CPD) could be agreed. This would detail what activities the member of staff needs to do to update their knowledge and skills, and by when (see Chapter 7).
- after an external quality assurance (EQA) visit. For example, an organisation was refused approval to offer a particular qualification during an EQA visit, as they did not have the required evidence to meet the criteria. The lead IQA developed an action plan to ensure the evidence was collated and ready by the date agreed with the EQA. This included having the required policies and procedures in place as well as staff members' original qualification certificates.

- after an internal quality assurance (IQA) sampling activity or a standardisation meeting. For example, agreeing relevant activities for individual assessors which relate to the content of the sample.

- after a classroom visit or deep dive activity. For example, a quality manager noted poor attendance of an adult Level I Functional Skills English group. The teacher explained that many of their learners worked in the care community and sometimes had difficulty attending classes due to shift patterns. An action plan was agreed with the teacher identifying how the content of any missed sessions would be caught up by the learners.

- preparing for an EQA visit or inspection. For example, allocating tasks such as assessors centralising CPD logs, policies and procedures, collating standardisation minutes, and identifying which IQA activities will take place in the future.

- during an EQA visit. For example, the EQA identified that one of the IQAs was providing verbal feedback to his assessors after a sampling activity, but not documenting what was said. An action plan was agreed as to how this could be formalised.

- to address any learner feedback concerns. For example, an online survey asked learners if they felt safe whilst training at college and 18% of learners stated they did not feel safe. The manager therefore developed an action plan which included sequenced tasks to enable them to understand why the learners didn't feel safe, followed by actions to address the learners' concerns.

- for learners as part of the review process or during feedback after an assessment activity. For example, a learner studying A level history has handed in an essay with poor spelling, punctuation and grammar (SPaG). To address this, the teacher has agreed an action plan with the learner to help improve her SPaG: this includes attending support classes weekly for the next two months, having a mentor to proofread her work, and attending a one-to-one tutorial session monthly with the teacher.

## Resources

- Action plan template

## Advantages

- Supports individuals or teams of people to improve their performance
- Gives a clear overview as to what needs doing and by when
- Helps to focus activities
- Can be individual, departmental, project or qualification driven

# Disadvantages

👎 Can be time-consuming to agree and document

👎 Actions must be monitored regularly and the plans updated

👎 Some staff might not take the process seriously

👎 Must be willing to follow up with capability (i.e. the ability/inability to meet job role expectations) or disciplinary action if staff are non-compliant

---

### Tip

When developing an action plan with an individual, ensure they understand the benefits of completing the tasks and how successful achievement will support them in their job role.

---

# Further reading and weblinks

Beardwell I & Holden L (1997) *Human Resource Management.* London: Pitman.

Crawshaw J et al. (2014) *Human Resource Management.* London: SAGE Publications.

Gravells A (2016) *Principles and Practices of Quality Assurance.* London: Learning Matters.

OpenLearnCreate – *Ten characteristics of a good action plan* –https://tinyurl.com/rgnpv5v

# 2 Allocating responsibilities to team members

| IQA activity | √ | EQA activity | √ | Deep dive activity | * |
|---|---|---|---|---|---|
| In person | √ | Remote | √ | Electronic/online | √ |
| Includes learners | | Includes assessors | √ | Includes others | √ |
| Promotes standardisation | | Lead IQA role | √ | Quality improvement role | √ |

*depends upon what and how you are planning to use the approach*

## What is it?

Allocating responsibilities will ensure the team members are working to their strengths, and fully understand what they need to do. To allocate roles and responsibilities for awarding organisation compliance, you should be a team leader, often referred to as a lead internal quality assurer (IQA). Similarly, for curriculum and quality improvements you should be a team leader or a manager (often known as quality managers/reviewers). You will need to determine who in your team is appropriately qualified and experienced to undertake the various tasks. This could be by asking them to carry out a SWOT analysis (see Chapter 46).

The number of learners, assessors and IQAs within your organisation will determine how the roles and responsibilities can be allocated to each member of your team. For example, a large organisation could have 20 or more full-time IQAs and five or more quality improvement roles, whereas a small provider may only have two part-time IQAs and one quality improvement role. Regardless of the number of IQAs or quality improvement roles within your organisation, it is vital that each member of the team knows and understands what their responsibilities are, how they should be carried out and when they must be completed by.

## What can it be used for?

It can be used to help allocate appropriate roles and responsibilities. Some large organisations often departmentalise the internal quality assurance process, for example a general further education college may have separate IQA teams for construction, motor mechanics, engineering, plumbing, business, travel and tourism, ESOL, hair and beauty, with a specialist subject lead IQA for each department. They often have a separate member of the senior leadership team who is ultimately responsible for the overall IQA process across the provision, as well as quality improvement, whereas a smaller provider may only have one IQA team with subject specialist IQAs, and a lead IQA who has knowledge and understanding of a range of subjects. The quality improvement person may oversee several departments, or there may be a quality manager/reviewer in each department depending on the size of provision.

Examples of IQA responsibilities which can be allocated to team members include:

- registering the learners for their qualification with an awarding organisation
- checking the registration details are correct, for example; the spelling of a learner name, and the qualification and unit combination they are working towards (before any assessment activity takes place). IQA and EQA samples should not take place if learners are not registered for their qualification
- sampling the induction process, gathering and following up learner feedback, whether it is positive or negative
- organising relevant and appropriate standardisation activities for assessors and other IQAs
- planning and undertaking sampling activities throughout the duration of the learner's time working towards the qualification
- providing developmental feedback to the assessor with an action plan for any areas which require improvement
- monitoring any awarding organisation changes or developments and sharing them with the team to ensure compliance
- mentoring and supporting new or inexperienced IQAs
- countersigning the decisions of unqualified IQAs
- tracking learner progress from start to finish against targets; interviewing learners, assessors and others who are involved in the learning process
- managing the EQA process including preparing for visits
- claiming certificates and ensuring learners receive the correct certificate for the qualification they have successfully achieved.

The lead IQA would usually agree the assessors' and other IQAs' caseloads based on their experience, and the distance they may have to travel to undertake their allocated tasks. However, some organisations have a senior member of staff who will allocate caseloads.

A quality improvement role will undertake an in-depth examination of the curriculum, known as a *deep dive*: this involves gathering a range of evidence regarding the curriculum intent; implementation and impact; and triangulating the findings.

Examples of responsibilities which a quality improvement person might undertake or could allocate to team members include:

- checking and monitoring that safeguarding practices are effective
- checking that the learning environment and resources are appropriate
- checking the curriculum design, for example, the sequencing of topics taught over time
- directly observing teaching, training and/or assessment in the workplace or a provider's premises: looking at learners' behaviours and attitudes towards their learning and personal development

- interviewing the learners, teachers or assessors over the telephone, online, or face to face to support the identification of progress over time
- monitoring learner attendance and punctuality
- monitoring the outcomes and destinations of learners
- scrutinising learners' work and feedback, usually with the learner or teacher present.

## Resources

- Documents, templates, proformas, records and logs (these may be paper based or electronic)
- Human resources, i.e. a team of IQAs or quality improvement people

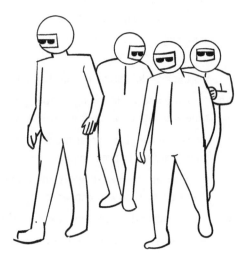

## Advantages

👍 Reduces the workload for each IQA or quality improvement person

👍 Tasks can be allocated to team members based on their strengths

## Disadvantages

👎 High risk of tasks not being completed by an individual

👎 Can cause confusion if team members do not fully understand their responsibilities

👎 The lead IQA or quality improvement person might feel the need to check everything carried out by their team members

### Tip

The lead IQA or quality improvement person could produce a visual document with each team member's tasks on, along with deadlines. This could be displayed in a staff office or on an online noticeboard. This will support individuals to know what they need to do and by when.

# Further reading and weblinks

Gravells A (2016) *Principles and Practices of Quality Assurance.* London: Learning Matters.

Ofsted (2019) *Inspecting the Curriculum: Revising inspection methodology to support the education inspection framework* – https://tinyurl.com/y3xkgnhm

# 3 Checking for plagiarism, fraud and malpractice

| IQA activity | √ | EQA activity | √ | Deep dive activity | * |
|---|---|---|---|---|---|
| In person | √ | Remote | * | Electronic/online | √ |
| Informal | | Formal | √ | Includes others | √ |
| Promotes standardisation | √ | Quality Assurance | √ | Quality Improvement role | √ |

*depends upon what and how you are planning to use the approach

## What is it?

Plagiarism is the practice of taking or using someone else's work or ideas and claiming them as your own. For example; copying text word-for-word from a book or internet site and not identifying, acknowledging or referencing correctly where the text came from. Plagiarism is classed as fraud; other examples of fraud include cheating in tests or exams, having others write assignments and claiming them as your own, incorrectly signing a document, or someone else signing your name as though they are you. Most educational organisations use the term malpractice to include plagiarism, fraud and cheating.

Quality assurance protects the risk of malpractice happening by undertaking specific processes to check the authenticity of assessed work. If you are working with regulated qualifications, there will also be guidance available from the awarding organisation.

You have a responsibility to ensure learners have been educated about plagiarism and fraud. To do this you need to help them to know and understand what it is and how to avoid it. For example, a learner studying history might be asked to research and write an essay on the fall of Rome. A Google search on the *Fall of the Roman Empire* brings up thousands of pages of information, some relevant and some not. A learner might in innocence copy and paste the information in its entirety or in sections into their own work, resulting in a serious allegation of fraud, leading to disciplinary action.

Prior to undertaking any assessment or setting any tasks, learners must be trained about plagiarism and fraud, including what it is and how to avoid it. In addition, regular reminders should be in place to ensure learners have retained the knowledge in their long-term memory.

## What can it be used for?

It can be used to ensure that the assessment process checks the authenticity of a learner's work, and that the quality assurance process routinely checks that this is happening correctly.

Examples could include:

- a learner is requested to sign a declaration stating that all work is their own
- a face-to-face observation takes place to assess a learner's skills, although photographic evidence has been submitted as part of the evidence
- an assessor checks the authenticity of their learner's work by asking them questions about the content of an essay they have submitted
- a learner must show photographic identity prior to a written or online examination.

Examples of what may indicate malpractice include:

- changes in font and font size if the work has been word processed
- changes in handwriting styles if the work is handwritten
- changes in the flow of the text or the language used
- if you know the learner speaks in a certain way at a certain level, yet their written work does not reflect this
- inconsistency of a pen signature (known as a wet signature as it's physical not electronic)
- not being able to see the face of the person who is being assessed in videos, or photographs being used for the majority of evidence
- spelling, grammar and punctuation are different from those of previously produced work
- the use of correction fluid to change words, dates or signatures.

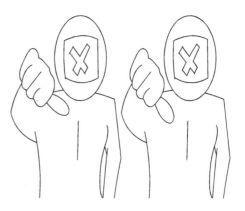

There are online plagiarism checkers that enable you to attach a file, or copy and paste word-processed text into a set field which will check the authenticity of work, highlighting any areas of concern. Some online plagiarism checkers can be downloaded for free, but they often have a limit on how many words you can enter.

## Resources

- A reliable method of checking the authenticity of learners' work

## Advantages

 Protects the integrity of the qualification

Protects the organisation's reputation

Ensures the learners have learnt what they have claimed to

# Disadvantages

🖒 Teachers or assessors may feel pressured to pass learners' work due to funding implications, targets and time constraints

🖒 It can be time-consuming to carry out checks

---

### Tip

Teaching learners about correct referencing techniques such as the Harvard referencing system or the scientific referencing system will help to prevent malpractice. Regular checks on learners' understanding of plagiarism and fraud, and its ramifications, keep it at the forefront of their minds, giving them less of an incentive to cheat.

---

# Further reading and weblinks

Gravells A (2016) *Principles and Practices of Quality Assurance*. London: Learning Matters.

Mansell S (2020) *50 Assessment Approaches: Simple, Easy and Effective Ways to Assess Learners*. London: SAGE Publications.

Ofqual – *Authenticity* – https://tinyurl.com/td8vcvz

Plagiarism – *About plagiarism* – www.plagiarism.org

University of Oxford – *Plagiarism* – https://tinyurl.com/zj7zafk

# 4 Coaching and mentoring others

| IQA activity | √ | EQA activity | √ | Deep dive activity | |
|---|---|---|---|---|---|
| In person | √ | Remote | | Electronic/online | * |
| Includes learners | | Includes assessors | * | Includes others | √ |
| Promotes standardisation | | Lead IQA role | √ | Quality improvement role | √ |

*depends upon what and how you are planning to use the approach*

## What is it?

Coaching and mentoring others is about supporting relevant colleagues to perform their job role to the best of their ability, and to become as independent and autonomous as possible. Both roles require patience and good communication skills, and enable a professional working relationship to be built up over time.

You could think of coaching as providing practical training in the short term, and mentoring about providing advice and support in the long term. It's a good idea to carry out an induction and initial assessment, and to agree a few ground rules when you begin to coach or mentor someone.

Coaching and mentoring could occur spontaneously as the need arises, or be planned for set dates and times. Both can be formal or informal, however it's useful to keep records of what was discussed and achieved.

## What can it be used for?

It can be used to coach more than one person at the same time to support them to develop their skills, knowledge and understanding. For example: you might identify that two new assessors need help regarding how to complete a particular document, and so you arrange to demonstrate this to them both at the same time.

Mentoring is usually carried out on a one-to-one basis and relates to knowledge and understanding. For example, if your role is an internal quality assurer (IQA), you will countersign the decisions of an unqualified IQA until they gain their qualification. Countersigning isn't just about checking what the IQA has done, it's also about supporting them on a long-term basis until they are confident and qualified. You could therefore decide to meet regularly with the IQA and agree an action plan (see Chapter 1). At each meeting, you can ask them to talk you through what they have been doing and then update the action plan. You therefore become a source of expertise and an impartial listener, providing advice and guidance to help them explore issues for themselves.

Generally, members of staff progress more quickly if they are allocated a coach or a mentor. This is because the coach/mentor can facilitate access to different experiences, activities and people which a member of staff might not normally come across. However, members of staff may become dependent or reliant on the coach/mentor and not think things through for themselves. They might also need support when the coach/mentor is not available, or disagree with what they have been asked to do. Hopefully, issues like this will not arise if the working relationship is open and honest.

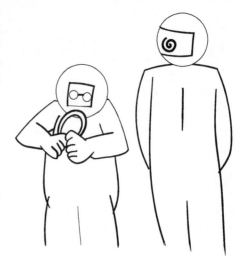

## Resources

- Relevant people
- Appropriate system for keeping a record of what was agreed and achieved

## Advantages

👍 The member of staff has someone to go to if they have any concerns, or just need someone to talk to

👍 The pace and approach of learning and support can be geared towards the needs of the member of staff

## Disadvantages

👎 It can be time-consuming

👎 The coach/mentor and the member of staff might not get on

👎 The coach/mentor might resent the member of staff for the amount of time they take up

---

### Tip

Never assume someone knows or can do something, always ask them before telling them, and then build on what you find out.

---

# Further reading and weblinks

*Coaching and mentoring* – https://tinyurl.com/ydh3tkvf

Lancer et al. (2016) *Techniques for Coaching and Mentoring.* New York: Routledge.

Garvey et al. (2017) *Coaching and Mentoring: Theory and Practice.* London: SAGE Publications.

Parsloe E & Leedham M (2016) *Coaching and Mentoring: Practical Techniques for Developing Learning and Performance.* London: Kogan Page.

# 5 Communicating with a team

| IQA activity | √ | EQA activity | √ | Deep dive activity | |
|---|---|---|---|---|---|
| In person | √ | Remote | √ | Electronic/online | √ |
| Includes learners | | Includes assessors | * | Includes others | √ |
| Promotes standardisation | | Lead IQA role | √ | Quality improvement role | √ |

*depends upon what and how you are planning to use the approach

## What is it?

Communicating with a team is all about being effective as a team leader or a manager. The four skills of language are *speaking, listening, reading* and *writing*. Different methods of communication can be used depending upon the situation or the person, for example:

- e-mail, texts or social networking – to quickly pass on information to the full team
- face to face – for meetings or staff appraisals (in person or online)
- intranet, web or cloud platform – for access to updated documents, policies and procedures
- newsletters – for bulletins and updates (hard copy or electronic)
- notice boards – for displaying workplans (see Chapter 49) and information for staff
- telephone – a call to check on a team member's progress
- written – for letters, memos, reports and minutes (hard copy or electronic).

Informal communications, i.e. speaking verbally in passing, can be more personal and may be quicker if you need to ask your team members to react immediately to some new information. However, not having a written record could prove to be a problem if a team member has no recollection of you asking them to do something.

## What can it be used for?

Communicating well with your team can influence the way your team members work, how they act and react, and how they perform their job role.

You will need to use the most suitable method of communication for a particular situation and person. In some cases, more than one method of communication may be necessary. For example; you might have an informal discussion with a team member and follow this up with an e-mail to confirm what was discussed. Formal meetings (see Chapter 25) should always be followed up with a written record.

The way you communicate with your team might be influenced by your personality. For example, you might prefer to use e-mails rather than the telephone. When using written communication, be aware that people might misinterpret your tone as negative when you meant it to be positive. Whichever method you use, you will need to make sure that what you convey is understood and acted upon by everyone.

You might not be liked by all your team members (or vice versa), however you are performing a professional role and you are not at work to be everyone's friend. Don't take it personally if you feel someone doesn't like you; it's probably the situation they don't like rather than you as a person. Always be professional and never allow your personal feelings to influence how you communicate with your team.

It's good to be aware of your verbal and non-verbal body language, e.g. not folding your arms when speaking as this could look defensive. You also need to take into account the way you speak and act, as your mannerisms might be misinterpreted by others.

There are many theories of communication, such as:

- Bandler and Grinder's Neuro Linguistic Programming (NLP) which is a model of interpersonal communication concerned with relationships and experiences. *Inter*personal skills are those which take place *between people*, in contrast to *intra*personal skills which are *within a person*. The model can be useful when providing feedback to staff to help influence their development.

- Berne's Transactional Analysis (TA) which is a method of analysing communications between people. Berne identified three personality states within people – the *child*, the *parent* and the *adult* – and he called them *ego states*. People behave and exist in a mixture of these states due to their past experiences and the situation they are in at the time. You might see this with other colleagues who take on a different ego state, for example; acting like a child when asking for help from you, yet acting like an adult with their peers.

## Resources

- Relevant people

## Advantages

👍 Knowledge of the theory of communication can help to improve how people work together

# Disadvantages

👎 If you don't deal effectively with situations when they occur, further issues could arise

👎 Some people can easily misinterpret something which is not communicated clearly

👎 No record of informal communications

---

### Tip

Try not to seem in a rush if someone needs to talk to you urgently. If you don't have the time straight away, arrange a time for as soon as you can. Try and be a *listener* rather than a *talker* when possible.

---

# Further reading and weblinks

*Bandler and Grinder's NLP* – https://tinyurl.com/yd6wkup2

Berne E (2016) *Games People Play: The Psychology of Human Relationships*. London: Penguin Books.

*Berne's Transactional Analysis* – https://tinyurl.com/586org

*Communication skills* – https://tinyurl.com/ybrnbrys

King P (2019) *Improve Your People Skills*: independently published.

# 6 Completing awarding organisation reports

| IQA activity | | EQA activity | √ | Deep dive activity | |
|---|---|---|---|---|---|
| In person | √ | Remote | √ | Electronic/online | √ |
| Includes learners | * | Includes assessors | * | Includes others | * |
| Promotes standardisation | * | Lead IQA role | | Quality improvement role | |

*depends upon what and how you are planning to use the approach*

## What is it?

If you are an external quality assurer (EQA) working on behalf of an awarding organisation (AO), you will be required to complete a report for each type of activity you undertake. Your AO will provide you with a report template which should be completed during, or shortly after you carry out any sampling and monitoring activities. The activities will be based on the plan which you will have sent your centre in advance, and could be carried out in person or electronically.

Report forms will differ between AOs and the activities to be carried out. You will need to fully understand the requirements of the qualification and the questions on the report, prior to completing it. To ensure a consistent approach, you should be given training (sometimes carried out as part of AO standardisation activities) regarding how to complete the report, the amount of detail to be added, how to make an objective decision, and when and how a copy will be given to the centre. You should also be familiar with the *Ofqual Handbook: General Conditions of Recognition* which are the rules and guidance for AOs and regulated qualifications.

Try not to get so engrossed completing the report that you don't allow enough time to carry out the activities on your plan, or to talk to and provide feedback to the centre staff.

## What can it be used for?

Report forms can be used to document:

- the approval of a centre to become accredited with an awarding organisation, i.e. to check staffing, resources, quality systems, assessment processes and learner support
- the approval of a centre to offer particular qualifications and levels
- the sampling and monitoring of learner, assessor and IQA activity within a centre (during a visit or remotely)

- a centre's quality assurance systems, policies and procedures
- the advice, guidance and support provided by the EQA to centre staff, perhaps as part of a developmental visit rather than a monitoring visit.

The report form will probably be electronic, allowing you to key in text into various areas, but not allowing you to change the questions. You should answer all the questions objectively, based on facts and not on your opinions. You should check for spelling and grammar errors to ensure your report is completed professionally.

The report will require you to make a decision based on risk, i.e. low, medium or high. For example, have your activities led you to make any action or improvement points? Action points are based on not following the explicit requirements to offer a qualification and to operate as an accredited centre. If an action point is not met, the centre will be sanctioned higher, i.e. from low to medium. An improvement point or recommendation is general advice to help and support the centre, but is not sanctionable.

Your AO will give you guidance as to how to reach decisions. If you find anything serious, you should contact your AO straight away, rather than discuss it with the centre, for example, plagiarism or fraud. All action points should be SMART: specific, measurable, achievable, relevant and time bound.

In most cases, you should discuss your decision with the centre staff and agree suitable target dates for all action points. You must be able to back up any statements in your report, in case there is a query, a complaint or an appeal by the centre. In some cases, the AO might require you not to discuss your decision, but will provide guidance as to what you should do.

Once you have completed the report, you should forward it to the AO within the required timescale, and inform your centre how and when they will receive their copy. If there are any action points, you should follow these up with the centre on a regular basis.

## Resources

- Report template from the awarding organisation (paper based or electronic)
- Suitable device or laptop on which to complete the report
- Telephone (in case you need to contact the AO)
- Your own records, i.e. to document interviews with centre staff, or for observing practice

## Advantages

- Provides an accurate and auditable record of activities, decisions, feedback, and action points
- Confirms to a centre that they are meeting the requirements (or not)

# Disadvantages

- Can be time-consuming to complete
- Can distract you from the activities which you must carry out
- You could become complacent when completing some aspects of the report if you are familiar with the centre staff and how they operate
- You might not want to sanction a centre as you know the centre will lose funding; you must remain objective
- The staff could be very persuasive, or you might feel threatened if you have to give a sanction: contact your AO if this happens before you finalise the report

---

## Tip

Look at the centre's previous report prior to your next activity with them. Contact them well in advance to check for any changes, such as staffing and resources, so that you are well prepared for what you might find. Remember to maintain confidentiality, and to evaluate your practice afterwards.

---

# Further reading and weblinks

Ann Gravells – *External quality assurance* – https://tinyurl.com/v4at54b

Gravells A (2016) *Principles and Practices of Quality Assurance*. London: Learning Matters.

*Ofqual Handbook: General Conditions of Recognition* – https://tinyurl.com/y9cydms6

*Plagiarism: About plagiarism* – https://www.plagiarism.org/

Read H (2012) *The Best Quality Assurer's Guide*. Bideford: Read On Publications.

# 7 Completing continuing professional development activities

| Internal activity | √ | External activity | √ | Deep dive activity | * |
|---|---|---|---|---|---|
| In person | √ | Remote | √ | Electronic/online | √ |
| Includes learners | | Includes assessors | √ | Includes others | * |
| Promotes standardisation | √ | Lead IQA role | √ | Quality improvement role | |

*depends upon what and how you are planning to use the approach*

## What is it?

Continuing professional development (CPD) is the term used to describe the activities you will need to complete to keep your professional skills, behaviours, attitudes, knowledge and understanding up to date. CPD activities are also used to upskill or reskill individuals, for example; a teacher delivering Level 2 in Carpentry would usually hold a Level 3 in Carpentry. Alternatively, if the teacher achieved a vocational qualification several years ago, they might need to spend some time in the industry to gain current experience, and to reskill themselves regarding any sector changes. It's worth checking the requirements regarding the qualifications and experience which are required for your particular subject. If the qualification is accredited via an awarding organisation (AO), this information can usually be found in their qualification specification for the particular subject.

CPD could relate to the vocational or academic subject you teach, or to pedagogical development to improve your teaching, assessment and quality assurance skills. It could also link to updating your knowledge regarding changes in legislation, regulations, codes of practice, policies and procedures, or revisions to qualifications or standards.

Activities could include:

- achieving specific qualifications
- participating in online forums and reading/writing blogs
- attending seminars or conferences (in person or online)
- attending standardisation activities and meetings
- attending workshops or lectures (in person or online)
- carrying out peer observations, shadowing colleagues and providing feedback
- coaching and mentoring others

- partaking in webinars or e-learning
- partaking in work experience placements in your own industry area, or a secondment or voluntary work
- reading and research
- reviewing textbooks
- sharing best practice.

# What can it be used for?

CPD can help you to reflect, review and improve your knowledge and practice. It could form part of an action plan (see Chapter 1) and be discussed during an appraisal meeting. It is usually planned and agreed with the lead IQA or your line manager, and is individual to you. If your employer is paying for a course or allowing you time away from your usual duties, it is likely that the CPD you are undertaking is for the benefit of the organisation as well as for you. You may be asked to sign a contract to agree that if you leave the organisation within a set period of time, you will be required to repay some or all of the money back.

The date of activity and a log of CPD hours should be maintained. The log should also detail the type of activity and the impact on your current and future practice, i.e. how it relates to the subjects taught/assessed/quality assured, or how it improves your job role. The log might also be sampled by the IQA or a quality reviewer to ensure the CPD undertaken is having the desired positive impact on you and the organisation.

External regulators such as awarding organisations or external inspectors may request to see samples of CPD logs and evidence of impact on learners, as part of their monitoring activities.

# Resources

- A means of documenting the CPD activities
- Access to relevant and meaningful CPD activities
- Qualification specification

# Advantages

- 👍 Supports credibility of staff and their organisation
- 👍 Helps keep staff up to date with their professional skills, behaviours, attitudes, knowledge and understanding
- 👍 Can support career progression
- 👍 Supports keeping the standards of the organisation high and consistent

# Disadvantages

🖓 Must be monitored or sampled regularly

🖓 Some staff may wish to include training for personal gain that won't benefit the organisation

🖓 Not all organisations will pay for CPD activities

🖓 May have to be carried out in own time

---

Tip

Developing a standardised template for individuals to document their CPD hours and activities will help with the sampling process, as all logs will be set out in the same format. It is useful to leave an area on the template for the member of staff to reflect on their development.

---

# Further reading and weblinks

Ann Gravells – *Continuing Professional Development (CPD)* – https://tinyurl.com/qvjoerh

College.jobs.ac.uk – *Continuing Professional Development (CPD) in Further Education* – https://tinyurl.com/ro4d2yn

Society for Education – *CPD* – https://tinyurl.com/h9qx395

The CPD Certification Service – *CPD* – https://tinyurl.com/vbta2fc

# 8 Completing quality assurance records

| IQA activity | √ | EQA activity | √ | Deep dive activity | * |
|---|---|---|---|---|---|
| In person | √ | Remote | √ | Electronic/online | √ |
| Includes learners | * | Includes assessors | * | Includes others | * |
| Promotes standardisation | √ | Lead IQA role | √ | Quality improvement role | * |

*depends upon what and how you are planning to use the approach*

## What is it?

Completing quality assurance records is part of the role of an internal or an external quality assurer (IQA/EQA). Records must be completed to evidence the activities which have taken place. Awarding organisations (AOs) will need to see them at some point, and the content must meet the requirements of the AO and of your own organisation.

Many of the completed records will be based on using pre-prepared documents and templates (see Chapter 13) which are either created in your organisation, or supplied by the relevant AO. This helps to ensure the standardisation of practice between staff who need to complete the same records.

## What can it be used for?

Records can be used to document various quality assurance activities, such as:

- discussions with learners
- discussions with witnesses and employers from the workplace
- feedback to assessors
- IQA planning, sampling and tracking
- observations of teachers, trainers and assessors
- responses to appeals and complaints
- standardisation of practice, such as the interpretation of qualification content
- team meetings.

When completing the records, whether you do this manually (i.e. by writing) or electronically, you must be factual, honest and accurate with your comments and responses. Most records will have open questions for you to answer with qualitative responses, or closed questions for you to answer *yes* or *no* which are quantitative responses. If you need to create an action point, ensure it is SMART: specific, measurable, achievable, relevant and time bound.

If you are unsure of how to respond to a question, you must ask for advice from a manager or someone appropriate who can help you. All records should be dated and signed (either paper based or electronically).

If you are completing paper-based records and you make a mistake, cross out the error and write above it. Do not use correction fluid as an inspector or auditor might wonder if you are hiding something. If you are using electronic records, you could save them with different version numbers as you update them.

Records will usually need to be kept for a set period, for example, three years. They should be the original records (if paper-based copies are used), not photocopies or carbon copies as they are easier to forge. Keeping the originals will ensure your records are authentic.

You will need to make relevant records available to any authorised persons who have a legitimate interest, such as funding auditors or external inspectors.

When documents and templates are reviewed or updated (see Chapter 38), all staff will need to be informed of the latest version. Further training might be required as to how to complete them.

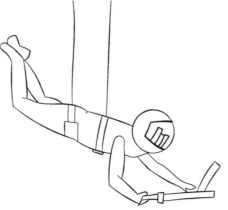

Records must always be kept safe and secure; your car boot or a shelf at home is not a good idea, nor is a corner of the staffroom or in an open-plan office. All records should comply with your organisation's requirements such as confidentially, and any relevant regulations and legislation such as data protection. Lockable filing cabinets or password protected electronic files should be appropriate.

## Resources

- Relevant documents and templates
- Suitable device or laptop on which to complete electronic records

## Advantages

👍 Provides auditable records

👍 Ensures staff can standardise their practice

## Disadvantages

👎 Some staff might use older versions of a particular document (if they are completed manually) as they have photocopied their own supply

## Tip

When completing a record which will be used to provide feedback to someone, make your comments genuine and supportive. For example, if you have carried out an observation of an assessor, write your feedback in the first person, be specific and don't use stock phrases.

# Further reading and weblinks

*Data Protection Act (1998)* – https://tinyurl.com/2c26dx8

Gravells A (2016) *Principles and Practices of Quality Assurance*. London: Learning Matters.

# 9 Creating a bank of assessment questions and exemplar answers

| IQA activity | √ | EQA activity | | Deep dive activity | |
|---|---|---|---|---|---|
| In person | √ | Remote | √ | Electronic/online | √ |
| Includes learners | | Includes assessors | √ | Includes others | * |
| Promotes standardisation | √ | Lead IQA role | * | Quality improvement role | |

*depends upon what and how you are planning to use the approach*

## What is it?

A bank of assessment questions will ensure all staff are being fair and equitable with their learners, when assessing the same areas. Having a set of exemplar answers will act like a guide to ensure all assessors are looking for similar responses from their learners to the questions. Assessment questions are a way of testing knowledge and understanding towards a particular topic, subject or qualification. There might be several teachers and assessors who are involved in the same subject area but with different learners, and a bank of questions and answers will help to save time and standardise practice.

If there is only one teacher or assessor for a subject, having a bank of assessment questions and exemplar answers will help them plan ahead to have the materials ready for when they are needed.

The materials can be amended and/or updated as necessary, however all staff accessing them will need to ensure they are using the latest version.

## What can it be used for?

Assessment is a fundamental way of checking that learning has taken place. This could be by the use of written or oral questions, assignments, essay questions, worksheets or another suitable method. In some cases, the awarding organisation (AO) might provide the questions but not the exemplar answers. If this is the case, the assessor/s should create suitable answers as a guide for marking.

Meetings could take place of teams of staff for particular subjects or qualifications to ensure a standardised approach to both the question content and the expected responses.

The assessment activities might be initial, formative or summative, and they might or might not be based on a formal qualification or a programme of learning. If the questions are to be used to formally assess learning, then they must be based on the relevant criteria.

This might be part of a qualification specification supplied by an awarding organisation, a programme handbook or an apprenticeship standard.

Question writing is a skill in itself, as there are many different ways of asking something. It could be that the questions will require short answers, or they could be essay type which require responses to be referenced.

If you are using the same questions with different learners at different times, be careful as they may collude and share their answers with each other. A way around this would be to have a master set of say 50 questions and responses, and randomly choose 20 each time.

## Resources

- Qualification specification, programme handbook or apprenticeship standard
- Method of creating the questions and exemplar answers, e.g. writing materials or suitable electronic software or apps

## Advantages

- 👍 Helps to standardise practice across assessors
- 👍 Enables the forward planning of assessment activities to save time as the course progresses
- 👍 Makes assessment quicker as you know what you are looking for
- 👍 Pre-prepared questions can be easily accessed and amended/updated as necessary

## Disadvantages

- 👎 Assessors must keep up to date with the latest version after any amendments have taken place
- 👎 Unscrupulous learners might be able to access the exemplar answers and adapt them to submit as their own responses

---

### Tip

If you think a learner has managed to access an exemplar answer, or copied an answer from another learner or via the internet, key in a few of their words into an online search engine and see what appears. Alternatively, ask your learner to talk through their answer. If they speak in a different way to how their written work looks, this should alert you to the fact that something may not be right.

---

# Further reading and weblinks

Gravells A (2016) *Principles and Practices of Assessment*. London: Learning Matters.

Ofqual – *Authenticity* – https://tinyurl.com/td8vcvz

Plagiarism – *About plagiarism* – www.plagiarism.org

# 10 Creating and updating policies and procedures

| IQA activity | √ | EQA activity | | Deep dive activity | |
|---|---|---|---|---|---|
| In person | √ | Remote | | Electronic/online | √ |
| Includes learners | | Includes assessors | * | Includes others | * |
| Promotes standardisation | √ | Lead IQA role | √ | Quality improvement role | √ |

*depends upon what and how you are planning to use the approach*

## What is it?

Policies and procedures are formal documents relating to responsibilities and activities which are carried out in, or carried out by staff at your organisation. They are designed to influence and control decisions and actions, and the boundaries in which they should be carried out.

A policy outlines the purpose, it is a statement of intent designed to prompt, assure, declare or comply with certain responsibilities or activities undertaken by staff at your organisation. It outlines the rules or standards of a desired outcome.

A procedure is the detailed method of how the policy is implemented. It should state who will do what, when and how. For example; a complaints policy would outline what would constitute as a complaint, whereas the procedure would explain how and when the complaint will be dealt with. Generally, policies do not change very often but procedures should be checked and updated at least annually.

Your role might involve updating policies and procedures, or creating new ones. Things to consider when creating new policies are:

1. identifying a need for the policy

2. involving people who have expertise of the area you are focusing on

3. gathering the required information to write the policy

4. drafting the policy

5. consulting with relevant staff

6. considering if the policy requires a procedure

7. considering how often the policy and procedure require updating or reviewing

8. finalising and gaining internal approval from the organisation for the policy and procedure

9.  implementing the policy and procedure and training staff

10. ensuring the policy and procedure is accessible by all staff, either paper based or electronically.

If you are involved in creating new policies and procedures, you should make a list of responsibilities and activities which you and your team undertake, and consider which ones require formal direction. For example, if you are involved in quality improvement you might introduce policies and procedures based on learner voice feedback activities, e-safety, and use of social networks during sessions. If you are an internal quality assurer you might introduce a policy and procedure regarding examinations, such as controlled assessment.

When a policy and/or a procedure is updated, all staff will need to be aware of the changes, and they might require some training. Previous versions will need to be removed from access.

# What can it be used for?

Policies and procedures, if used and followed correctly, are a fantastic tool to protect everyone involved in the organisation. They give clear guidance on what a person should or shouldn't do in a given situation.

Examples of policies and procedures that can be used in an educational setting include (in alphabetical order):

*   anti-bullying
*   anti-malware
*   appeals
*   assessment
*   bribery
*   complaints
*   continuing professional development
*   data protection
*   deep dive
*   disciplinary
*   disclosure and barring service (DBS checks)
*   document retention
*   environment and sustainability
*   equality and diversity
*   e-safety
*   examinations (including access arrangements)
*   health and safety
*   internal quality assurance

- learner voice
- lone working
- malpractice (plagiarism, fraud, cheating, unfair means; see Chapter 3)
- observation of teaching, learning and assessment
- professional development reviews and appraisals
- safeguarding (including the Prevent Duty)
- social networking
- use of technology and security
- workplace stress.

## Resources

- Depends upon what approach and how you are planning to use it

## Advantages

👍 Provides instruction regarding how to perform a particular task

👍 Helps staff to make decisions effectively

👍 Protects staff from acting in a manner that may lead to a disciplinary hearing

👍 Enables staff to take responsibility without having to ask a manager what to do

## Disadvantages

👎 Relies on staff reading and understanding the policy and procedure

👎 Is dependent on staff following the latest version of the policy and procedure

👎 Can be time-consuming to write and update

---

### Tip

To support you to keep track of when policies and procedures are created and updated, you could include a footer on each document which is cross-referenced to a master list. The footer could include a policy reference code, i.e. the date it was created and when it was last reviewed. The master list could include the name of the person who approved it and when, the frequency of review and the name of the person responsible for the review, plus dates of previous and future reviews.

---

# Further reading and weblinks

DIY Committee Guide – *How to develop policies and procedures* – https://tinyurl.com/tscmhzx

Gravells A (2016) *Principles and Practices of Quality Assurance*. London: Learning Matters.

# 11    Creating job descriptions or role/person specifications

| IQA activity | √ | EQA activity | | Deep dive activity | |
|---|---|---|---|---|---|
| In person | √ | Remote | √ | Electronic/online | √ |
| Includes learners | | Includes assessors | * | Includes others | * |
| Promotes standardisation | | Quality Assurance | √ | Quality Improvement | √ |

*depends upon what and how you are planning to use the approach*

## What is it?

A job description or role/person specification is an internal document which states the requirements, duties, responsibilities and general tasks a person will be expected to carry out at work. It may also describe the required qualifications, competence, skills, behaviours, attitudes, knowledge and/or understanding required to perform a specific role. You should always set clear expectations from the start regarding what a person should be doing as part of their job role. This helps them perform to the best of their ability. What is essential and what is desirable for the post should be clearly stated. This will help you to reduce the number of unsuitable applicants.

It should be developed and implemented for anyone involved in a quality assurance (QA) or quality improvement (QI) role, i.e. lead internal quality assurers (IQAs), IQAs, quality managers or team leaders, teachers, assessors, witnesses, and support staff such as readers, invigilators or interpreters.

## What can it be used for?

A job description or role/person specification has multiple uses including:

- recruitment purposes: examples include a member of staff retiring or being promoted leaving a gap in the quality improvement or quality assurance team; an increase in learner numbers; or a change in qualifications offered may require additional IQAs. Using a job description or role/person specification when advertising a post will help to narrow the number of unsuitable applicants. It allows recruiters to compare evidence for each applicant against the job requirements, thus speeding up the recruitment process. It can also protect your organisation legally, as the job description or role/person specification can defend why an applicant was selected or not.

- measuring an individual's performance: examples include identifying any qualifications; continuing professional development (CPD); or training gaps. Also recognising those who go above and beyond their role, to enable best practice to be shared, or to support a promotion or pay rise; to identify those who are not meeting the job description or role/person specification requirements, or who are not performing to the agreed standards. It can be a key point of reference for disputes or disciplinary issues.

By defining roles, responsibilities and expectations through a job description or role/person specification, individuals have clarity about what they need to do. For example; the expectation of a lead IQA is to manage the IQA process from start to finish, whereas an IQA may only be required to undertake a small part in that process, such as sampling a particular unit. Or a quality improvement reviewer may write a whole organisation, department or section self-assessment review, whereas a teacher would be expected to complete a self-assessment review for their own sessions.

It can also be used to support standardisation as every person involved in the quality improvement or quality assurance activity will have a clear summary of what their expectations are. This helps to prevent individuals doing something that is someone else's job, wasting valuable time, or doing something wrong.

# Resources

- A standardised template for a structured layout
- Descriptions, specifications and requirements of the job role, along with responsibilities

# Advantages

- Clarifies the role and helps to set expectations
- Is a key point of reference
- Provides a structure
- Supports standardisation
- Can be used as a reference point for training and development, and for appraisals

# Disadvantages

- Can be limiting, as only a summary
- Reduces flexibility
- Might require regular updating if roles change

> **Tip**
>
> If you don't already have job descriptions or role/person specifications in place, you could discuss roles and responsibilities with your team. This will help to develop a document based on each individual's strengths, therefore outlining and formalising the required tasks you want them to do.

# Further reading and weblinks

Crawshaw J et al. (2014) *Human Resource Management*. London: SAGE Publications.

Gravells A (2016) *Principles and Practices of Quality Assurance*. London: Learning Matters..

The HR Booth – *What are the benefits of a job description?* – https://tinyurl.com/wsbyh3z

# 12 Dealing with appeals, complaints and disputes

| IQA activity | √ | EQA activity | √ | Deep dive activity | |
|---|---|---|---|---|---|
| In person | √ | Remote | √ | Electronic/online | √ |
| Includes learners | * | Includes assessors | * | Includes others | * |
| Promotes standardisation | √ | Lead IQA role | √ | Quality improvement role | √ |

*depends upon what and how you are planning to use the approach*

## What is it?

An appeal is usually initiated by a learner if they disagree with an assessment decision. For example; an assessor may fail a learner due to a lack of evidence, but the learner believes they have produced or demonstrated the required amount to meet the criteria. The learner could appeal against the assessor's decision.

A complaint is often about a situation or a person and can be initiated by a learner, a parent or someone else. For example; a learner may complain about a lack of suitable resources, a parent may complain about a lack of communication from your organisation with regard to their child's progress, or a member of the public may complain about information, advice and guidance in relation to accessing a course or a programme of study.

Disputes arise because one person thinks something is right, when another thinks it's not. For example, an assessor suspects a learner has plagiarised some text, but the learner states it's their own work. The organisation's plagiarism policy would need to be invoked, and it might transpire that the learner has just forgotten to reference the text in their work.

## What can it be used for?

Appeals and complaints are generally made when a person feels they have been treated unfairly or if they perceive something as bad practice. An appeal, if not handled correctly, could lead to a complaint which could escalate to a dispute. Having a complaints policy and appeals procedure that looks into concerns or issues and puts any mistakes right, will give your learners and others confidence in the decisions you make.

An appeals and complaints policy should aim to ensure that:

- making a complaint or appeal is as easy as possible
- the handling process complies with General Data Protection Regulations (GDPR)

- complaints or appeals are dealt with promptly, politely and when appropriate, confidentially
- complainants or appellants are listened to and treated with courtesy and empathy
- action to rectify the cause of the complaint or appeal is identified, implemented and evaluated
- no one is disadvantaged as a result of making a complaint or appeal
- complainants are kept informed of the progress and outcome.

An appeals procedure should be in place to formalise the process if an informal discussion does not reach a suitable outcome first. It should be divided into stages, for example, if a learner disagrees with an assessment decision, the procedure could be:

- stage one – formally speak to your assessor, if you still don't agree with the decision, move to stage two
- stage two – write to the internal quality assurer (IQA), if you still don't agree with the decision, move to stage three
- stage three – write a formal letter of appeal to the manager of the organisation.

Each stage should have a deadline, for example seven days. Templates could be used to standardise the process. If the qualification is regulated, the appeals procedure should also include a stage four with details of the external quality assurer (EQA) or awarding organisation.

A complaints policy should include how to complain, for example; formally in writing or informally verbally. Who the complaint should go to and the timescale of acknowledgment through to resolution should be included. It should also state what will not be constituted as a complaint. For example, it might state that a complaint in relation to an academic decision must go through the appeals procedure, or something that happened more than a certain time ago will not be looked at.

Appeals and complaints should always be handled promptly, fairly, consistently, and proportionately by working in an open and accountable way that builds trust and respect. All information should be documented to provide an audit trail.

Policies and procedures in any organisation are there to protect staff and learners. All staff should read and be trained on how to use the complaints policy and appeals procedure, with an emphasis that any complaint or appeal should not be taken personally.

## Resources

- Relevant policies and procedures
- Suitable templates

# Advantages

👍 Learners are confident to lodge an complaint or appeal

👍 Practices can be improved by monitoring trends from appeals and complaints

👍 Bad practice can be addressed and corrected

👍 EQA reports can identify that your organisation is being compliant with relevant policies and procedures

# Disadvantages

🗨 Policies and procedures must be regularly reviewed and updated, which can be time-consuming

🗨 All staff who are involved in the process must be trained to follow the policies and procedures, and to know about any updates

🗨 It can be difficult to get staff together for training or to check that all staff have read the policies and any updates

---

### Tip

When sharing the appeals procedure with learners, make sure you include names, e.g. rather than just write *formally speak to your assessor,* add the person's full name and contact details. This supports the learner to feel confident to follow up any of their concerns.

---

# Further reading and weblinks

Gravells A (2016) *Principles and Practices of Quality Assurance.* London: Learning Matters.

Lifehack – *7 steps for resolving customer complaints* – https://tinyurl.com/tpfas6t

Ofqual – *Complaints procedure* – https://tinyurl.com/nzwnug3

# 13 Designing and updating quality documents and templates

| IQA activity | √ | EQA activity | √ | Deep dive activity | √ |
|---|---|---|---|---|---|
| In person | √ | Remote | √ | Electronic/online | √ |
| Includes learners | √ | Includes assessors | √ | Includes others | √ |
| Promotes standardisation | √ | Lead IQA role | √ | Quality improvement role | √ |

## What is it?

A document or template is a pre-formatted record which highlights the areas that you should focus on. It usually includes specific formatting with areas that a person cannot change, and areas that they can add text, numbers or diagrams to. Electronic software applications of document templates might include predetermined drop-down lists for you to select from, or a paper version might have text which can be chosen by underlining or circling.

Your organisation may already have quality documents and templates in place and your role might be to review and update them. In contrast you may have to design and create them for your team to use.

Examples of quality improvement and quality assurance documents that benefit from having a standardised template are:

- action plans
- agendas for meetings
- assessment records, i.e. decisions, feedback to learners, and tracking
- awarding organisation certificate claims
- awarding organisation registration of learners
- checklists for various activities, e.g. appraisals
- continuing professional development (CPD) records
- curriculum vitaes (CVs)
- external quality assurance (EQA) reports and action plans
- induction documents
- IQA feedback to assessor records
- learner progress and achievement tracking records

- learner review audits
- learning walk records
- observation of teaching, learning and assessment checklists
- peer reviews or observations
- professional development reviews
- records of internal quality assurance (IQA) activities
- risk assessments
- risk registers
- safeguarding reports
- sample plans
- self-assessment reports (SAR)
- single central records (for safeguarding compliance)
- standardisation records.

Whether you are designing or updating documents or templates, try to keep the layout as simple as possible and consider the following points:

- what is the intended use and how much information do you need?
- what order do you want the information in? The information, where possible, should flow in a logical sequence which will help the person who is completing it
- is the document going to be completed manually or via an electronic device? This will affect the design of the template. If the document is paper based consider how much space will be required to hand write the information in each area (known as a field)
- what information do you need to include to enable a person to be able to complete the sections you require?

Your document or template should have a professional appearance (perhaps with the organisation's logo on) and be checked thoroughly for any spelling, punctuation and/or grammatical mistakes. A record should be kept of the name of the document, the date it was created, who created it, and the version number (this could also be included as a footer). When it is reviewed or updated, staff should be informed, and any older versions destroyed or removed from access.

## What can it be used for?

Quality improvement and quality assurance both benefit from having a consistent approach to the completion of documents and templates. Every member of the team will be able to complete them following the same format, which supports standardisation of practice.

A well-designed document or template gives staff a starting point and a framework as to what and how they should complete them for a particular task. It also saves time for the person extracting the required information as they are following the same layout for all the different responses.

# Resources

- Software which enables you to design or update a document or template, such as a word processor, specialist programs or apps
- Printing facilities (if applicable)

# Advantages

- Helps to promote standardisation
- Staff can review each other's completed documents to ensure they are completing them correctly
- Can reduce time, as only the required fields are completed
- Gives a starting point and a framework to the person completing the document
- Easier to review the completed document if a consistent approach is used

# Disadvantages

- Can be time-consuming to design
- Requires regular reviewing and updating
- Some staff might use older versions of a particular document as they have photocopied their own supply, or might not know they have been updated

---

### Tip

When you design or update a document or template, it is always useful to ask a colleague to proofread it and let you know if the text flows logically, if it will be straightforward to complete, and if there are any spelling, punctuation and/or grammatical errors.

---

# Further reading and weblinks

Gravells A (2016) *Principles and Practices of Quality Assurance*. London: Learning Matters.

# 14   Designing questionnaires and surveys

| IQA activity | √ | EQA activity | √ | Deep dive activity | √ |
|---|---|---|---|---|---|
| In person | √ | Remote | √ | Electronic/online | √ |
| Includes learners | √ | Includes assessors | √ | Includes others | √ |
| Promotes standardisation | √ | Lead IQA role | √ | Quality improvement role | √ |

## What is it?

A questionnaire is a method of gathering qualitative information and data which is usually descriptive, as the respondents must answer open, probing, recall and process questions. For example:

1.  open questioning (*How would you …?*) – questions are posed to the respondent that cannot be answered by a simple *yes* or *no*.

2.  probing questions (*Why exactly was that?*) – often used after asking an open question to encourage the respondent to explore their initial answer further and to give more details or information.

3.  recall and process questioning (*How did you …?*) – questions are set around a particular job or task which requires the respondent to remember and consider specific information before answering.

A survey is a method of gathering quantitative information and data which is used to measure the satisfaction levels of something. Survey results are generally measured by numerical results, e.g. *95% of learners agreed their assessor was supportive*. Survey questions are usually *closed* or *true* or *false* questions which require the respondent to select a pre-set answer. For example:

1.  closed questioning (*Would you …?*) – questions are posed to the respondent which can be answered by a *yes* or *no* response or a *strongly agree, agree, neither agree or disagree, disagree,* or *strongly disagree* response, or by circling a smiley face (☺  ☺  ☹). These types of responses don't demonstrate understanding, and the respondent often chooses a middle option if they are unsure which way to go.

2.  true or false – only one of the responses can be correct.

You may decide to combine the questionnaire and survey together, giving you the opportunity to gather qualitative and quantitative information and data at the same time.

When designing your questionnaire or survey you will need to consider who your respondents are, what you are hoping to find out or measure, and why. The questions should be written in a language and level appropriate to your respondents, and a set date given for the return of the responses. If you are planning to issue a questionnaire to a large amount of people, it would be wise to pilot a small amount first. This would allow you to test your questioning techniques, and to ensure the questions are valid and reliable.

# What can it be used for?

Questionnaires and surveys are both massively useful ways of formally gathering feedback from those involved in the teaching, learning and assessment process.

After analysing the responses received, you should create an action plan to address any relevant points, and write a report of your findings to share with your team. If any changes will take place as a result, for example; improving a particular service for learners, then those learners should be notified.

For example, an internal quality assurer (IQA) used a questionnaire to gather information regarding the learners' assessment process using the following questions:

1.  Explain your involvement in developing your assessment plan.

2.  What type of assessment activity was used and why?

3.  How did your assessor provide feedback to you?

4.  If you could change one thing in relation to the assessment process, what would it be?

The IQA was able to use the responses from the learners to identify specific training needs for the team of assessors and set appropriate action plans. A report was produced for the senior manager.

A further example is where a quality reviewer used a survey to measure the satisfaction levels of groups of learners just after their induction onto a learning programme. They used the following questions, each with an *agree* or a *disagree* response:

1.  I am receiving the help and support I need.

2.  I feel safe and secure whilst learning.

3.  The facilities and resources are good.

4.  I was able to join the right course for me.

5.  At the time I enrolled, it was made clear what I would be doing during the course.

6.  The first few weeks of my course were well organised.

The quality reviewer was able to identify from the results that the majority of the respondents disagreed that the first few weeks of their course were well organised. The quality reviewer then designed a questionnaire based on what happens in the first few weeks of a learner starting their programme. This was then used to gather qualitative information and help to identify exactly what the problems were so that they could be rectified.

## Resources

- A pre-prepared questionnaire or survey

## Advantages

👍 Can be carried out remotely (using online media which ensures confidentiality)

👍 Can collect a large amount of responses

👍 Questions can be designed to meet a specific area for concern

👍 Most online questionnaires and surveys can automatically analyse results

## Disadvantages

👎 Respondents may not answer truthfully (they might give an answer that they think is expected, so as not to displease)

👎 May have a low response rate

👎 Depending upon how it is implemented, the feedback might not be confidential

---

### Tip

If questionnaires or surveys are responded to anonymously, respondents are more likely to give an honest answer. Always set a target date for their completion.

---

## Further reading and weblinks

Gravells A (2016) *Principles and Practices of Quality Assurance.* London: Learning Matters.

MSG – *Questionnaire design* – https://tinyurl.com/ycexsa9z

Survey Monkey – *Use education surveys to gain academic insights* – https://tinyurl.com/wo65z8y

# 15 Devising a quality assurance rationale

| IQA activity | √ | EQA activity | √ | Deep dive activity | |
|---|---|---|---|---|---|
| In person | | Remote | | Electronic/online | |
| Includes learners | | Includes assessors | | Includes others | √ |
| Promotes standardisation | √ | Lead IQA role | √ | Quality improvement role | |

## What is it?

A quality assurance rationale is a statement relating to *why* quality assurance must take place within an organisation. The rationale will help maintain the credibility of the products and services offered, as well as the reputation of your organisation. It doesn't have to be long, perhaps three or four sentences, but all staff must be aware of its existence.

Having a rationale will help ensure all quality assurance activities are robust, and that they are safe, valid, fair and reliable. It should follow the ethos of the organisation to ensure that quality assurance activities are managed and implemented properly. It might form part of the quality assurance policy (see Chapter 10).

Once the rationale has been produced, a *strategy* must be written for each qualification and/or programme of learning. This will state how theory is put into practice (see Chapter 16).

## What can it be used for?

It can be used by external quality assurers (EQA) for the centres they will monitor, and is generally produced by the awarding organisation. The EQA will use it as a basis to formulate their strategy for each of their centres.

It can be used by internal quality assurers (IQA) as a basis for creating their strategy and sampling plans (see Chapter 28). It is generally produced by the lead IQA or quality manager. However, it should be discussed with all staff to ensure they agree with it and will follow it.

---

### Example of an internal quality assurance rationale:

*All internal quality assurance activities will comply with internal and external organisations' requirements to assure the quality of assessment for all learners. All assessment decisions*

*(Continued)*

(Continued)

*will be carried out by qualified assessors in each subject area and sampled by qualified internal quality assurers. This will ensure the safety, fairness, validity and reliability of assessment methods and decisions. It will also uphold the credibility of the qualification, and the reputation of the organisation.*

## Resources

- Quality assurance policy and an understanding of the organisation's ethos
- Awarding organisation's guidance for operating as a centre

## Advantages

👍 Ensures all staff are aware of the ethos of the organisation

👍 Supports EQAs to produce their centre monitoring strategies

👍 Supports IQAs to produce their strategy and sampling plans

## Disadvantages

👎 Although it doesn't have to be long, it can take time to get it right

👎 A lead IQA or quality manager might produce it without collaborating with their team, therefore imposing their own values, which others might not agree with

### Tip

Before you create a rationale, find out if one already exists. It might just need updating.

## Further reading and weblinks

Ann Gravells – *External quality assurance* – https://tinyurl.com/v4at54b

Ann Gravells – *Internal quality assurance* – https://tinyurl.com/ybydj7ol

Gravells A (2016) *Principles and Practices of Quality Assurance*. London: Learning Matters.

Read H (2012) *The Best Quality Assurer's Guide*. Bideford: Read On Publications.

# 16 Devising a quality assurance strategy

| Internal activity | √ | External activity | √ | Deep dive activity | |
| In person | | Remote | | Electronic/online | |
| Includes learners | | Includes assessors | | Includes others | √ |
| Promotes standardisation | √ | Lead IQA role | √ | Quality improvement role | |

## What is it?

A quality assurance strategy is a statement of all the activities, monitoring and sampling which you will perform (either as an internal or an external quality assurer) for a particular qualification or programme of learning. It should be based on the rationale (see Chapter 15) as well as any identified risk factors (see Chapter 24).

Having a strategy will help you to plan what will be monitored and when, and ensure that your quality systems are fit for purpose. If you are quality assuring an accredited qualification, it will be a requirement of the awarding organisation (AO) that you have a strategy in place.

You will need to refer to the qualification specification or programme handbook to ascertain any particular requirements. For example, if the AO requires you to sample certain aspects in a given timescale.

## What can it be used for?

It can be used by an external quality assurer (EQA) to plan what activities they will carry out with their centres and why.

It can be used by internal quality assurers (IQA) to plan what they will sample, how and when.

The strategy should be regularly reviewed and updated, particularly in the light of staffing changes and/or qualification and programme updates. Feedback received from inspections and reports can also influence the strategy.

The strategy might be produced by the lead IQA or quality manager, or it might be your responsibility to write it for your particular subject. However, it should be discussed with your team to ensure they are familiar with it.

## Example of an internal quality assurance strategy:

*IQA strategy for Level 2 Customer Service (one internal quality assurer, four assessors, 100 learners):*

*The IQA will:*

- *observe each assessor every six months, this will be in different locations to cover all assessment methods (new assessors will be observed more as necessary)*
- *talk to a sample of learners and witnesses*
- *sample at least five assessed units from each assessor across a mix of learners (new assessors will have a higher sample rate)*
- *chair a bi-monthly team meeting*
- *facilitate regular standardisation activities to cover all units over a period of time*
- *maintain full records of all IQA activities*
- *liaise with the EQA and implement external quality assurance action points.*

The amount of detail you include in your strategy will be dependent upon the experience of your assessors and the types of activities you will carry out. When planning your strategy, you should take into account factors such as:

- assessment locations: on or off the job, college, training room or other environment

- assessment methods: are they robust, safe, valid, fair and reliable; are they complex and varied; do they include online assessments; are witnesses used; does holistic assessment track achievements across different units?

- assessors: availability for observations and meetings (some assessors could be located at a distance or have other jobs, can activities take place remotely online via the internet?); assessors' experience, qualifications, workload and caseload (experienced assessors could be sampled less than new assessors – but be aware of complacency)

- learners: location, full time/part time, ethnic origin, gender, specific needs (do assessors need to adapt any assessment methods for any particular learners' needs?)

- qualification or programme to be assessed: are assessors familiar with these; have assessors standardised their interpretation of them, is the content due to be revised; is there a risk of plagiarism or malpractice?

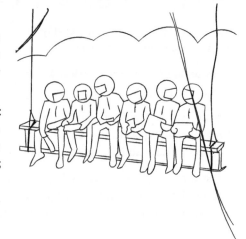

- types of records to be completed (paper based or electronic)

# Resources

- Quality assurance rationale
- Qualification specification or programme handbook for your particular subject
- Awarding organisation's guidance for operating as a centre

# Advantages

👍 Ensures all staff are aware of the activities which will take place

👍 Supports EQAs to plan what they will sample and why

👍 Supports IQAs to produce their sampling plans

# Disadvantages

👎 Although it doesn't have to be long, it can take time to get it right and must be regularly updated

👎 A lead IQA or quality manager might produce it without collaborating with their team, therefore staff might not be aware of it

> **Tip**
>
> Use the *who, what, when, where, why* and *how* model to help you prepare the content of your strategy.

# Further reading and weblinks

Ann Gravells – *External quality assurance* – https://tinyurl.com/v4at54b

Ann Gravells – *Internal quality assurance* – https://tinyurl.com/ybydj7ol

Gravells A (2016) *Principles and Practices of Quality Assurance*. London: Learning Matters.

Read H (2012) *The Best Quality Assurer's Guide*. Bideford: Read On Publications.

# 17 Following regulations and requirements

| IQA activity | √ | EQA activity | √ | Deep dive activity | * |
|---|---|---|---|---|---|
| In person | √ | Remote | | Electronic/online | √ |
| Includes learners | | Includes assessors | √ | Includes others | * |
| Promotes standardisation | √ | Lead IQA role | √ | Quality improvement role | √ |

*depends upon what and how you are planning to use the approach*

## What is it?

Following regulations and requirements is all about ensuring compliance with them. This will uphold the credibility of the qualifications and/or programmes you offer, as well as the reputation of your organisation.

Regulations are often called *rules* and they specify mandatory requirements which must be met. They are usually set by public bodies and government departments. For example, in education one of the regulators is Ofqual who regulate qualifications, examinations and assessments in England. Ofqual approves and regulates awarding organisations (AOs). A representative of an AO will visit to quality assure their accredited qualifications, if you offer them. There will also be specific regulations which relate to specialist subjects. For example; the Food Hygiene (England) Regulations (2006) for staff who deliver and assess catering subjects.

Requirements are usually set by organisations and agencies. For example, Ofsted, who inspect funded provision in England. If you receive government funding for educational programmes, your organisation will be inspected by a representative from Ofsted at some point.

Requirements can include those set by your organisation, for example; codes of practice, policies and procedures. They may, or may not be mandatory, and it might be your role to produce and/or review and update them. They can also be set by professional bodies for their members, such as the Society for Education and Training's Code of Professional Practice.

## What can it be used for?

Once you are aware of the relevant regulations and requirements your staff need to follow, you will be able to support them by providing relevant up-to-date advice and guidance. This will help to ensure they are performing their role correctly, and that they are remaining compliant.

It might be useful to create an up-to-date list of the relevant regulations and requirements which your staff must follow. This can include generic and subject specific aspects such as:

- awarding organisation's criteria for offering their qualifications
- internal codes of practice such as lone working, disciplinary, conflict of interest
- internal policies and procedures such as assessment, quality assurance, appeals and complaints
- Ofqual's Handbook: General Conditions of Recognition
- Ofsted's Education Inspection Framework (EIF)
- relevant legislation such as the Data Protection Act (2018), and the Health and Safety at Work etc. Act (1974)
- relevant regulations such as Manual Handling Operations Regulations (1992).

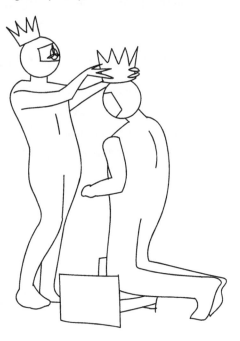

Discussing these at a team meeting, and having relevant documents and weblinks accessible, will help to ensure everyone is performing their role correctly.

## Resources

- A list of relevant regulations and requirements with up-to-date weblinks
- Hard copies or electronic copies of relevant regulations, codes of practice, policies and procedures

## Advantages

- Ensures all staff are performing their role correctly
- Maintains compliance with relevant requirements
- Helps support standardisation by ensuring all staff interpret the requirements in the same way

## Disadvantages

- Can be time-consuming to keep up to date with any changes, and convey these to staff
- Some staff might not be aware of a change and continue to operate to previous regulations or requirements

> **Tip**
>
> Don't be afraid to ask for help and advice if you are unsure of anything. This might simply be by asking a manager or a colleague to clarify something, or by contacting an external quality assurer for guidance with a particular area of a regulation.

# Further reading and weblinks

Legislation – https://www.legislation.gov.uk

Ofqual – https://tinyurl.com/o3bypv7

Ofsted – https://tinyurl.com/lczdnn8

Society for Education & Training – *Code of Professional Practice* – https://tinyurl.com/y8qavupy

# 18 Inducting new staff

| IQA activity | √ | EQA activity | | Deep dive activity | |
|---|---|---|---|---|---|
| In person | √ | Remote | * | Electronic/online | * |
| Includes learners | | Includes assessors | | Includes others | √ |
| Promotes standardisation | √ | Lead IQA role | √ | Quality improvement role | √ |

*depends upon what and how you are planning to use the approach*

## What is it?

An induction is the process of initially introducing a member of staff to your organisation, to other staff, and to their job role. If the induction is for a new member of staff (rather than an existing member of staff who has received a promotion) it will include an employment contract for the work that is going to be undertaken, and support regarding the following points:

- a training plan to meet the needs of the post
- acceptable working practices
- information technology access and computer logins
- initial targets or goals for the individual
- legal and statutory requirements
- organisational policies and procedures
- organisational structure
- organisational systems and processes
- the organisation's vision, mission and values.

If the induction is for an existing member of staff it might include an update to their employment contract for the additional work that will be undertaken. A training plan to support them to meet the requirements of the job role might also need to be agreed.

When starting a new job role, there is a lot of information for the member of staff to learn, and it is often easier to break the induction content into different stages, perhaps over a number of weeks or months. For example, prior to planning an induction process consider the following points:

- what do I want the member of staff to achieve during their first six weeks, their first four months and their first six months? (What are the key objectives you want them to achieve and by when?). The job description or role/person specification can be used (see Chapter 11)

- what does the member of staff need to know, understand and do, to carry out their job effectively?

- what support and training needs to be put in place to enable the member of staff to achieve their objectives within the timescales?

Once you have decided the key objectives you want the member of staff to achieve, you can plan the induction content. For example, a new assessor's induction could be broken into four stages.

Stage 1 (within the first few days)

Provide the new assessor with a welcome pack – this could be paper based or electronic and include:

- a welcome note from the principal or head of department
- any forms which need to be completed such as next of kin details
- a glossary of terms to help the assessor understand relevant jargon
- an organisation chart to enable the assessor to know how they fit into the structure of the company
- key policies, procedures and working practices which the assessor needs to quickly familiarise themself with
- the organisation's vision, mission and values.

The welcome pack could also include details about systems and processes including information technology access and any login details that are required to access the internal systems. It could also include information relating to any mandatory training such as safeguarding or general data protection regulations.

Once the assessor has the welcome pack, a one-to-one meeting should take place to agree the objectives that the assessor must meet, and a training plan agreed to support them to meet their objectives. Long-term objectives should be agreed for the period of the induction (e.g. six months), with milestones to measure the progress made. Objectives for a new assessor might include that they work towards a relevant assessment qualification, and attend regular team meetings and standardisation activities. A mentor or buddy could also be provided to support the assessor throughout the induction process.

Stage 2 (within the first six weeks) and Stage 3 (within the first four months)

Meet with the assessor to check their progress towards their objectives. Check if there have been any issues or problems, identify if there are any further training requirements and update the training plan accordingly, and agree new milestones towards the objectives.

Stage 4 (within the first six months)

This is the final stage of the induction process and the assessor should now be familiar with the working practices, and have fully met their objectives which were agreed at stage 1. The assessor should be ready to be signed off from their induction, however if the assessor has not met their objectives, the induction period could be extended.

It is helpful to track the progress of a new member of staff. An induction checklist detailing the main points of the induction will support you to do this, as will keeping notes from your meetings.

# What can it be used for?

An induction can be used for staff new to the organisation or for existing staff moving into a new role.

A structured induction for new members of staff can be used to ensure legal and statutory requirements are adhered to, that the member of staff knows and understands the expectations of the organisation, and what their job role requires. It helps to identify any training requirements or needs, and it supports staff to become productive and efficient as quickly as possible.

# Resources

• An induction checklist

# Advantages

🖒 Can help to reduce staff turnover by motivating and encouraging the member of staff

🖒 Can support the organisation's efficiency and productivity

🖒 Can help the new member of staff to feel valued and respected

🖒 Provides all the necessary information for the member of staff to perform their job role successfully

🖒 Sets clear expectations from the start

# Disadvantages

🖓 Can be time-consuming to plan and carry out

🖓 Is reliant on the person who is carrying out the induction to put time and effort into supporting the staff member

> **Tip**
>
> Once the induction period is over, the member of staff should be offered ongoing support and training to further develop themselves. Dates for regular reviews and appraisals can be agreed.

# Further reading and weblinks

ACAS – *Checklist for induction of new staff* – https://tinyurl.com/uqtj6b5

ACAS – *Starting staff induction* https://tinyurl.com/rslexem

Imperial College London – *New Staff induction pack material* – https://tinyurl.com/slacyrr

# 19 Interpreting the content of qualifications, programmes and standards

| IQA activity | √ | EQA activity | √ | Deep dive activity | * |
|---|---|---|---|---|---|
| In person | √ | Remote | √ | Electronic/online | √ |
| Includes learners | | Includes assessors | √ | Includes others | * |
| Promotes standardisation | √ | Lead IQA role | √ | Quality improvement role | √ |

*depends upon what and how you are planning to use the approach

## What is it?

Interpreting the content of qualifications, programmes and standards is all about making sure everyone who teaches, assesses and quality assures them, knows and understands what is required.

Qualifications are usually offered by an awarding organisation (AO) who will issue a certificate to successful learners. They will provide a *qualification specification* or *programme handbook* which should state how each subject should be assessed and quality assured. It is usually available from the AOs website. It will provide information and guidance in the form of an *assessment strategy*. This should state the qualifications, experience and professional development which teachers, assessors and internal quality assurers should have. It will also state how the subject should be assessed, and whether assessment activities are provided, or if you need to create your own.

Apprenticeship programmes will also have requirements which staff must meet regarding their qualifications and experience. It might be part of your role to ensure these are met when interviewing new staff. Details can be found in the relevant apprenticeship standard.

Your organisation might offer non-accredited qualifications or bespoke courses, which are known as programmes of learning. These do not lead to a formal qualification or a certificate issued by an AO. However, you could design and issue a record of attendance, or a certificate of achievement to give to successful learners.

Standards can include those set by employers for their staff (perhaps as part of a job specification), those set by standard setting bodies (SSBs) for industry-related qualifications, or those for apprenticeship programmes. They can also include those set by professional bodies such as the Education and Training Foundation's Professional Standards for Teachers and Trainers.

# What can it be used for?

Interpreting the requirements of qualifications, programmes and standards will ensure all staff who are involved with them are standardising their approaches and practice. This will give a consistent service to learners. It will also make sure they understand and apply the content correctly. For example; a particular unit could be misinterpreted in some way, leading to assessors using different assessment methods. Regular meetings, standardisation and updates to staff will help ensure a consistent approach is adhered to, and ensure everyone is up to date with relevant requirements.

It might be your role to apply the assessment strategies for the accredited qualifications your organisation offers. This will include checking the qualifications and experience of your staff to meet the requirements as stated in each subject specific qualification specification. Continuing professional development (CPD) might be a requirement of the strategy (see Chapter 7). For example, a retail skills teacher might need to work a certain number of hours in the sector to maintain their currency of practice. You will need to maintain records of how each member of staff meets the requirements, for external inspection and quality assurance purposes.

# Resources

- Qualification specification, programme handbook or apprenticeship standard
- Records of how staff meet the relevant assessment strategies

# Advantages

- Ensures all staff are meeting relevant requirements
- Helps support standardisation by ensuring all staff interpret the requirements in the same way

# Disadvantages

- Can be time-consuming to keep up to date with any changes and convey these to staff
- Some staff might not be aware of a change and continue to operate to previous requirements
- Staff might not always take ownership of their CPD

## Tip

The content of qualifications, programmes and standards is regularly updated. Make sure you keep up to date with the relevant AO and sector/subject specific websites and discuss upcoming changes with your team as soon as possible. Make a note of the last dates for registration and certification of regulated qualifications so that you move over to the new content straight away.

# Further reading and weblinks

Federation for Industry Sector Skills and Standards – https://fisss.org/

Federation of Awarding Bodies – https://awarding.org.uk/

Gravells A (2016) *Principles and Practices of Assessment*. London: Learning Matters.

Institute for Apprenticeships – https://tinyurl.com/y72vvt9q

# 20 Interviewing prospective staff

| IQA activity | √ | EQA activity | | Deep dive activity | |
|---|---|---|---|---|---|
| In person | √ | Remote | * | Electronic/online | * |
| Includes learners | * | Includes assessors | * | Includes others | * |
| Promotes standardisation | * | Lead IQA role | √ | Quality improvement role | √ |

*depends upon what and how you are planning to use the approach

## What is it?

Interviewing prospective staff to join your team might be because you:

- are delivering a new qualification that requires staff with particular experience and/or qualifications that your current team members do not have
- have a member of your current team who is ill, due to retire, has been promoted, or is leaving the organisation
- have a rise in learner numbers and need to increase the team
- have identified an expertise gap in your current team
- are contingency planning and want to train new assessors, internal quality assurers or quality improvement personnel.

Advertising the post either internally or externally, with a concise job description or role specification (see Chapter 11) which details the essential and desirable requirements, will help you reduce the number of unsuitable applicants.

Once the post has been advertised, and application forms received, the selection process can begin. Each applicant's details should be measured against the job description or role specification to ensure they meet the essential requirements listed. The desirable requirements can be used to condense the number of applicants you take forward to interview.

Interviews can be held in different contexts, i.e. traditional interviews are held face to face between the applicant and the interviewer, who asks a series of questions. The risk of a one-to-one interview is that the interviewer could be biased, a small panel interview could therefore be used to reduce this. Alternatively, telephone and online visual interviews have become increasingly popular over recent years. Whichever context the interview takes place, it is important the process is based around the competence, skills, behaviours, attitudes, knowledge and/or understanding required of the applicant to perform the job role.

For example, interviewing a potential internal quality assurer (IQA) could also include:

- a face-to-face panel interview with questions based on the experience and qualifications of the IQA
- a simulated desk-based task to internally quality assure an assessor's decision and provide written feedback
- a problem-solving exercise, such as developing an action plan to support a new assessor
- a short micro-teach session by a prospective teacher to a small group of learners.

You may decide to involve others in the interview process. For example, a potential quality manager could be asked to observe a teacher delivering a session. Feedback from the teacher and learners would support other interview activities by indicating the applicant's communication skills, behaviour and attitude.

In addition to interview activities, the applicant's credentials and right to work must be verified. If the interview is face to face they should bring with them their:

- national insurance number (if from the UK) or right to work documents
- proof of address
- proof of identity
- original qualification certificates.

If the applicant is new to the organisation, references from previous employers will help to support the selection process.

# What can it be used for?

Interviewing prospective staff supports you to evaluate the suitability of each applicant for the particular job role advertised. Meeting face to face and questioning an applicant will help you see what they are really like in person, compared to their written application. It will also support you to identify other skills the applicant may have, such as organisational skills (how well did they plan and prepare for the interview?), their ability to work under pressure (how did they respond to direct questioning?) and their personality (will they fit in with the culture of the organisation?).

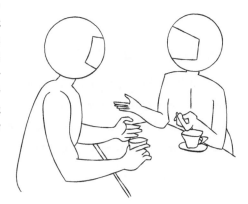

# Resources

- Job description
- Role specification
- Pre-prepared questions to ask the applicant

- Relevant activities for the applicant to carry out
- Online communication method if not interviewing face to face

# Advantages

Supports you in verifying the information on the application form

Helps you assess the applicant's interpersonal and communication skills

Face-to-face interviews enable you to see other indicators such as body language, facial expressions and other non-verbal cues

# Disadvantages

Applicants may be anxious and not perform to their best ability

Applicants may be dishonest during the interview

First impressions can often be wrong

---

### Tip

If the applicant is going to be working with children or vulnerable adults, it may be necessary to have checks carried out by the Disclosure and Barring Service (DBS) prior to them commencing work. To save time, you could ask applicants to complete the DBS form in advance and bring it with them to the interview, along with the necessary original identity documents to enable you to verify them and take a copy. The successful applicant's completed DBS form can be immediately sent away once a decision is made as to their suitability for the role, and the others can be securely disposed of.

---

# Further reading and weblinks

Beardwell I & Holden L (1997) *Human Resource Management*. London: Pitman Publishing.

Crawshaw J et al. (2014) *Human Resource Management*. London: SAGE Publications.

Gravells A (2016) *Principles and Practices of Quality Assurance*. London: Learning Matters.

Disclosure and Barring Service – https://tinyurl.com/ceydl2w

# 21  Keeping and maintaining records

| IQA activity | √ | EQA activity | √ | Deep dive activity | |
|---|---|---|---|---|---|
| In person | √ | Remote | √ | Electronic/online | √ |
| Includes learners | | Includes assessors | √ | Includes others | √ |
| Promotes standardisation | | Lead IQA role | √ | Quality improvement role | √ |

## What is it?

Your organisation will need to keep and maintain certain records and information about its employees, learners and others, to allow it to deal with numerous aspects of the business. This includes monitoring recruitment, attendance, performance and achievements, as well as aspects relating to health and safety, equality and diversity, and safeguarding. It is also necessary to process certain information so that staff can be recruited and paid, courses planned, and legal obligations to funding bodies and the government complied with.

Records should always be accurate, detailed, up to date and legible. Whether the records are paper based or electronic, they should be signed and dated every time they are amended.

To comply with the law, information must be collected and used fairly, stored safely, and not disclosed to any other person unlawfully. To do this, you must comply with the Data Protection Act (2018) which incorporates the General Data Protection Regulations (GDPR). In summary, the Data Protection Act states that personal data shall:

- be obtained, processed fairly, and lawfully, and shall not be processed unless certain conditions are met
- be obtained for a specified and lawful purpose and shall not be processed in any manner incompatible with that purpose
- be adequate, relevant and not excessive for those purposes
- be accurate and kept up to date
- not be kept longer than is necessary for that purpose
- be processed in accordance with the data subject's rights
- be kept safe from unauthorised access, accidental loss or destruction
- not be transferred to a country outside the European Economic Area, unless that country has equivalent levels of protection for personal data.

All examination and assessment materials must be stored securely and in accordance with each awarding organisation's instructions. You must maintain the confidentiality of all learners' details and their responses to exam questions, to help prevent malpractice or fraud.

Secure storage could be by using a lockable filing cabinet or a safe, or password protected computer files. Awarding organisations usually give guidance on what is acceptable as well as the procedures for managing examination and assessment materials. For example, GCSE examination papers must only be released by your organisation's examinations officer, and handed to official invigilators who will take the papers to the examination room. After the examination, all the completed papers will be collected by the invigilator before the learners are allowed to leave the room, and then handed back to the examinations officer. The papers should be securely stored or packed into the envelopes supplied by the awarding organisation, and dispatched safely to them for external marking.

Use of information technology storage facilities is also subject to the provisions of the Data Protection Act (2018). Some *end-point assessment* and *functional skills* are examples of online tests and are subject to the same principles as paper-based examinations. Any records kept electronically should be backed up in case a file or document becomes corrupt. They should also be encrypted and password protected.

By law, any breaches or potential breaches of data security must be reported to your organisation's data protection officer who will report it to the appropriate regulatory authority. A *data breach* means a breach of security leading to the accidental or unlawful destruction, loss, alteration, unauthorised disclosure of, or access to, personal data transmitted, stored or otherwise processed.

In contrast, the Freedom of Information Act (2000) does enable certain information held by public authorities to be accessed by relevant people. This includes policies and procedures relating to human resource management, health and safety, and equality and diversity records and information.

# What can it be used for?

It may be necessary to share your records with an appropriate organisation, for example; a funding body, as evidence of the activities your own organisation has undertaken.

Records have a multitude of uses including:

- evidencing a case of malpractice or fraud
- evidencing activities during an inspection with regulatory authorities
- evidencing appeals and complaints
- improving performance
- keeping medical and contact information of learners and staff in case of an emergency
- meeting the requirements of an awarding organisation and your own organisation
- monitoring assessors' progress and development to ensure they are meeting relevant requirements

- providing evidence of staff records such as their qualifications, continuing professional development, or disclosure and barring service (DBS) number
- proving action points have been met from an internal or external inspection or monitoring process
- proving assessment and internal quality assurance activities have taken place
- proving learner attendance for funding bodies or regulatory authorities
- showing that feedback from question-naires and surveys has been considered when reviewing provision
- tracking enrolments, registrations and learner progress to support recruitment and achievement.

All records should be kept confidential and they should only be accessible to relevant staff and authorised visitors.

## Resources

- A data protection policy
- Secure storage facility, depending upon what records you are keeping or maintaining

## Advantages

- Following the requirements of the Data Protection Act (2018) will support you to keep and maintain your records correctly
- Keeping and maintaining records correctly enables you to provide the evidence required for legal, statutory or regulatory requirements

## Disadvantages

- Failure to comply with the general data protection requirements can have serious consequences for you and your organisation, including prosecution which can be costly

### Tip

Take the time to read your organisation's data protection policy and ensure you are keeping all records in accordance with it.

# Further reading and weblinks

*Data Protection Act (2018)* – https://tinyurl.com/yxb9wka7

Freedom of Information Act (2000) – https://tinyurl.com/2va4k6s

Gravells A (2016) *Principles and Practices of Quality Assurance.* London: Learning Matters.

ICO – Freedom of Information Act. Definition document for colleges and further education – https://tinyurl.com/wjpk99c

JCQ – *Joint Council for Qualifications* – https://tinyurl.com/twv7a7a

# 22 Making decisions when sampling evidence

| IQA activity | √ | EQA activity | √ | Deep dive activity | √ |
| In person | √ | Remote | √ | Electronic/online | √ |
| Includes learners | * | Includes assessors | * | Includes others | * |
| Promotes standardisation | √ | Lead IQA role | √ | Quality improvement role | |

*depends upon what and how you are planning to use the approach

## What is it?

Making decisions when sampling evidence is all about judging that assessors are performing their role competently when assessing their learners. This can be part of an internal and external quality assurance role. Besides observing assessors in practice, you can sample their assessment planning, decisions and feedback records. You can check the learner's work and ensure that everything meets the assessment requirements of the qualification specification, programme handbook or apprenticeship standard. All evidence should be valid, authentic, reliable, current and sufficient (VARCS).

When sampling learners' work, you are not re-assessing or re-marking it, but making a decision as to whether it meets the requirements. You are ensuring the assessor's plans and feedback records are documenting all the activities, and that their decisions are safe, valid, fair and reliable.

When sampling work from different assessors, if you are sampling the same aspects, you can see how consistent the different assessors are performing. You can then note any inconsistencies to discuss at the next team meeting. For example, if one assessor is giving more support to learners, expecting them to produce far more work than others, or observing them too much in the workplace, then this is clearly unfair.

As you are only sampling aspects of the assessment process, there will be some areas that get missed. This is a risk as you can't sample everything from everyone. You can always carry out an additional random sample at any time, and ask to see an aspect of assessor practice which isn't part of your original sampling plan (see Chapter 28). Your plan is a live document which can be amended at any time.

## What can it be used for?

It can be used to confirm (or not) if the learner has met the requirements, and if the assessor has supported them effectively, and maintained complete and accurate records.

You might agree with the assessor, in which case you can give them feedback as to what they have done well. You might agree, but feel the assessor could have given more developmental feedback to their learner. You can then give the assessor appropriate feedback as to how they could develop and improve their feedback skills. Alternatively, you might disagree with an assessor's decision and refer the work back to them. If this is the case, you would need to be very explicit as to why the work had not met the requirements, and give the assessor advice regarding how they can support their learner's achievement. This should all be documented, and a target date for completion agreed. Make sure you keep a note on your sample plan and tracking sheet (see Appendix 1) if any action is required, so that you can follow it up by the target date. Always update your records to reflect what was sampled and when, and what action has been met and when. A clear audit trail of all activities must be maintained to assist compliance and transparency. It also helps in the event of an appeal or a complaint.

You should compare different assessors' records to ensure they are completing them in a standardised way. For example, some assessors might be very brief with their feedback and others quite comprehensive. If this is the case, then the assessor who only writes brief comments might not be fully supporting their learner. You could take copies of some records, remove all names and use them during a standardisation meeting to agree a consistent approach.

If you have a concern when sampling the work of one assessor, you could sample more work from them for the same aspect, but with different learners, to see if it was a one-off. You could then sample the same unit from different assessors to see if there is a trend. If you find that other assessors are also having the same problems with the same aspect, it might be that they have all misinterpreted the same thing, therefore you will need to update them immediately. Otherwise, the learners might be disadvantaged due to no fault of their own. You could then schedule this particular area for a standardisation activity.

You should also be making decisions as to whether the assessment types and methods used are adequate, fair and appropriate. If one assessor is carrying out three observations with all their learners, but another is only carrying out one and relying on witness testimonies, then that is clearly not fair. If one assessor is expecting some learners to write a 2,000-word essay, and others a 1,500-word essay, then again, that's not fair.

Triangulating what you do by looking at the assessor's records; learners' evidence, and talking to learners and/or witnesses will help you make an objective, valid and reliable decision.

## Resources

- Qualification specification, programme handbook and/or relevant apprenticeship standard
- Learner evidence

- Evidence from others, e.g. witnesses in the workplace
- Completed assessment records
- Internal quality assurance templates
- Sampling plan and tracking sheet

# Advantages

👍 Enables you to ensure the assessors are performing their role effectively

# Disadvantages

👎 If you don't allow enough time to carry out a thorough sample, you might make an incorrect decision

👎 If accurate records are not maintained as to how you reached your decisions, there could be an appeal, and you might not remember all the facts afterwards

---

### Tip

After a period of sampling, analyse your findings and provide overall generic feedback to the assessors.

---

# Further reading and weblinks

Gravells A (2016) *Principles and Practices of Quality Assurance*. London: Learning Matters.

Wood J & Dickinson J (2011) Quality Assurance and Evaluation in the Lifelong Learning Sector. Exeter: Learning Matters.

# 23 Managing a team

| IQA activity | √ | EQA activity | √ | Deep dive activity | |
|---|---|---|---|---|---|
| In person | √ | Remote | √ | Electronic/online | |
| Includes learners | √ | Includes assessors | √ | Includes others | |
| Promotes standardisation | * | Lead IQA role | √ | Quality improvement role | √ |

*depends upon what and how you are planning to use the approach

## What is it?

Managing a team is all about ensuring the people you are responsible for are working effectively together. A team is a group of individuals who have different ideas and ways of performing, but who share a common goal. Whether you are working in quality improvement or quality assurance, it is highly likely as part of your role that you will be managing a team.

A quality improvement team could include:

- heads of curriculum, departments, centres or sites
- mentors and coaches
- observers
- support assistants
- teachers and trainers.

A quality assurance team could include:

- assessors
- internal quality assurers (IQA)
- teachers and trainers
- witnesses in the workplace.

To manage a successful team, you will need to consider the aims and key objectives you need to achieve. Before allocating roles and responsibilities to each person in your team, ask each them to complete a SWOT analysis (see Chapter 46) to support you to identify individual strengths and weaknesses. Once you have identified an individual's strengths, you can allocate appropriate responsibilities (see Chapter 2). Each team member should be inducted into their role (see Chapter 18) and a training plan agreed for any areas identified as requiring improvement.

It is beneficial to carry out appraisals with each member of your team. This could be conducted formally at least once a year, however professional dialogues and conversations should be ongoing throughout the year. Appraisals should provide the opportunity for a two-way discussion to:

- assess performance from the previous year towards the staff member's role and responsibilities, including performance objectives and any relevant standards
- agree expectations for the year ahead by reviewing and agreeing appropriate performance objectives
- confirm timescales for achievement of the objectives, and where necessary, for provision of support, including development
- ensure staff understand what they are being measured towards, i.e. the performance criteria, including any relevant professional standards and any other appropriate evidence which needs to be taken into account when reviewing their performance, including any potential barriers to success
- discuss and agree appropriate monitoring arrangements and any other support, including observations of their practice, analysis of retention and achievement data, learner numbers and feedback (if appropriate to their role)
- agree any areas of relevant training and development and related action points
- allow the member of staff to raise any issues or concerns regarding their workload or work/life balance, and any potential barriers to success.

You will need to use different communication methods and techniques to influence the way your team members work (see Chapter 5). The way you communicate can affect their morale and motivation, which could impact on the team's performance.

# What can it be used for?

It can be used to improve and build upon working relationships. Your role as a team leader or a manager is centred around people and professional relationships. Staff who feel valued and respected perform better than those who don't.

Key points which can help to support an effective team include:

- acknowledging good work
- delegating the right tasks to the right people
- developing positive working relationships
- focusing on aims and/or key objectives
- having honest, open and consistent conversations
- leading by example
- managing any conflict immediately.

There are many theories regarding how to manage teams and team behaviours, and these include Belbin, Gardner and Tuckman:

- Belbin's Team Roles is about the way people behave in groups. Belbin identified nine clusters of behaviour, each of which is termed a *team role*. Each team role has a combination of strengths they contribute to the team, and allowable weaknesses. It's important to accept that people have weaknesses, therefore if you can focus on their strengths you will be able to help manage their weaknesses. Knowing that individuals within teams take on different roles will help you to manage your team members effectively.

- Gardner's Emotional Intelligence (EI) is a behavioural model, the principles of which provide a new way to understand and assess people's behaviour, attitudes, interpersonal skills, management styles and potential. This could be useful if you have a large team of staff who aren't always working in a consistent manner.

- Tuckman: the forming, storming, norming and performing model is about the way a team develops maturity and ability as relationships are established. Tuckman later added a fifth stage to his theory called adjourning which relates to people's wellbeing, but does not relate directly to managing and developing a team.

# Resources

- Relevant people

# Advantages

👍 Supports the achievement of aims and objectives

👍 Can increase motivation and productivity

👍 Can help people to work together more effectively

# Disadvantages

👎 Individuals can cause problems if any issues are not dealt with immediately

---

**Tip**

If you are involved with reviewing or appraising teachers and trainers in your team, you could use the Education and Training Foundation's Professional Standards for Teachers and Trainers as a basis for aspiration and discussion.

---

# Further reading and weblinks

Belbin's Team Roles – https://tinyurl.com/y9nzfcdh

BusinessBalls – *Tuckman's Forming, Storming, Norming, Performing Model* –https://tinyurl.com/y3yy6s4q

Education and Training Foundation's Professional Standards for Teachers and Trainers – https://tinyurl.com/yad3l8s8

Verywellmind – *Gardner's Emotional Intelligence (EI)* – https://tinyurl.com/y7sjc39d

# 24 Managing risks and contingency planning

| IQA activity | √ | EQA activity | √ | Deep dive activity | √ |
|---|---|---|---|---|---|
| In person | √ | Remote | * | Electronic/online | * |
| Includes learners | | Includes assessors | √ | Includes others | * |
| Promotes standardisation | | Lead IQA role | √ | Quality improvement role | √ |

*depends upon what and how you are planning to use the approach

## What is it?

Managing risks and having contingency plans in place will help to prevent or reduce any potential issues. Aside from health and safety and safeguarding, there are many risk factors that could disadvantage a learner or an organisation. Recognising potential risks by identifying critical functions of your organisation will support you to respond to potential issues. Each function should be risk assessed, and where possible, a plan put in place to reduce or mitigate the risk. Where it is not possible to reduce or mitigate a risk, a contingency plan should be developed. The plan will list critical activities which need to take place.

Business critical functions could include what to do in the event of:

- communication failure
- data storage failure or a breach of data protection
- lack of equipment, resources and supplies
- multiple instances of staff absence at the same time
- premises incident, e.g. fire, failure of water, power, heating or ventilation
- reduced access, e.g. the lockdown of buildings, towns or cities.

Each of the points should be considered and a procedure developed regarding how each failed function will impact on teaching, learning and assessment. For example, if there is an issue with a building which cannot be accessed by staff or learners, a contingency plan could be to re-locate to different premises for an interim period. If a procedure is in place to ensure a stock-take is regularly undertaken, the risk of running out of equipment, resources and supplies is reduced, as long as a timely order is put in to replace them. Good human resource management should reduce the risk of multiple staff absences. However, a contingency plan to have a bank of qualified and trained sessional or freelance staff who can be called in at short notice, would alleviate the problem.

As well as *business* critical functions there are *teaching, learning and assessment* critical functions that should also be considered.

These include but are not limited to:

- having appropriately qualified, experienced and competent teachers, assessors and internal quality assurers. They should be able to interpret the qualification criteria and assessment requirements and support learners to progress through their qualification

- having the correct ratio of teachers and assessors to learners, including having adequate time to carry out all assessment requirements, for example; travelling to work placements, marking and assessing learner work, and providing constructive and developmental feedback

- carrying out regular standardisation activities

- ensuring learners are registered for the right course for their needs, including the application process and use of initial and diagnostic assessments to facilitate this

- encouraging learners to be motivated, confident and open to the teaching, learning and assessment process

- setting appropriate targets and formalising action plans and tutorial reviews

- maintaining records of attendance, progress and achievement

- completing all actions by the target date from previous external visits or inspections

- having suitable environments for delivery and assessment to take place

- having appropriate secure storage and procedures to prevent improper access to examination and assessment materials

- ensuring all staff are trained regarding organisational policies and procedures

- having appropriate equipment, resources and materials which support all activities

- registering learners with an awarding organisation in a timely manner, to ensure assessment decisions are valid

- utilising reliable and meaningful witness testimonies

- ensuring reliable and meaningful work placements for learners

- having appropriately trained staff to support learners who have learning difficulties and disabilities, including having the knowledge to apply for examination special arrangements and concessions

- planning assessment which is individual, meets the assessment requirements, and is timely

- ensuring learners produce evidence in a timely manner, which is valid, authentic, reliable, current and sufficient

- using suitable assessment types and methods to gather evidence of achievement.

Each point should be carefully considered and the risk managed by either putting a procedure in place to reduce the risk, or by contingency planning. You should also reflect on what other critical functions are imperative to the delivery and assessment of qualifications and/or programmes of learning.

# What can it be used for?

The assessment and management of risks and any subsequent contingency plans should be used to minimise disruption to your organisation, staff and learners.

Many of the teaching, learning and assessment critical functions listed can be managed, and the risk reduced by having:

- a clear internal quality assurance strategy

- an adequate sampling plan which is adhered to

- quality assurance activities and records which are maintained and reviewed

- action and training plans in place for teachers, trainers and assessors according to their needs

- feedback from learners, teachers, assessors and other stakeholders which is evaluated and acted upon

- a concise induction process for new staff

- a process for tracking learner progress.

Where a risk cannot be minimised, a contingency plan should be put in place, for example; a worldwide virus causes all training providers to stop delivering sessions face to face. The contingency plan is to deliver remotely to learners through distance learning activities. Teachers are therefore able to provide and authenticate the required theoretical written assignments which the teacher then marks and assesses. The teacher provides constructive and developmental feedback to the learner which supports them to improve for their future written assignment work. Learners could also be given mock tests to help prepare them for an apprenticeship end-point assessment. The internal quality assurer or quality reviewer can sample the quality of provision remotely. For example, by observing a session being delivered by video link or a webinar, by sampling learning packages and materials online, and by sampling assessment decisions and feedback electronically.

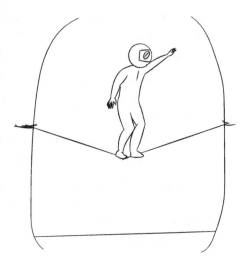

# Resources

- Depends upon what and how you are planning to use the approach

# Advantages

- Supports compliance with legislation and regulations
- Reassures staff and learners
- Minimises disruption to staff and learners
- Reduces the risk of disadvantaging a learner

# Disadvantages

- It can be difficult to identify all risks
- A contingency plan does not cover every scenario
- Can be time-consuming to plan for and process new procedures
- Staff training for the contingency activities needs to be undertaken
- Needs to be regularly updated

---

### Tip

Wherever possible, try to reduce or mitigate risks by following awarding organisation guidance as well as obeying statutory and regulatory requirements.

---

# Further reading and weblinks

Ann Gravells – *Risks to external quality assurance* – https://tinyurl.com/v4at54b

Ann Gravells – *Risks to internal quality assurance* – https://tinyurl.com/ybydj7ol

Gravells A (2016) *Principles and Practices of Quality Assurance.* London: Learning Matters.

MindTools – *Contingency planning* – https://tinyurl.com/hcd2ctx

# 25 Managing team meetings

| IQA activity | √ | EQA activity | | Deep dive activity | |
|---|---|---|---|---|---|
| In person | √ | Remote | √ | Electronic/online | √ |
| Includes learners | | Includes assessors | √ | Includes others | * |
| Promotes standardisation | √ | Lead IQA role | √ | Quality improvement role | √ |

*depends upon what and how you are planning to use the approach

## What is it?

Team meetings are an essential part of managing and maintaining the quality of your provision, i.e. the products and services you offer. Ideally, they should be planned a year in advance. For example, if your academic year runs from August to July, then dates of the team meetings should be added to the team members' diaries at the beginning of the year through to the end of the year. This ensures everyone knows when the meetings are and at what time, enabling them to plan their own time so that they can attend.

An agenda should be created detailing the key points and content that will be discussed or carried out during the meeting, and the name of the person who is going to be in charge of that point of the agenda. It is beneficial to circulate the agenda at least a week prior to the meeting, to enable all members of the team to be prepared. Depending on the methods of communication used in your organisation, the agenda could be sent via email, uploaded to the intranet, sent through the internal post, given by hand or posted.

Every organisation will hold their team meeting slightly differently depending on their size and numbers of staff. Some organisations hold team meetings by particular qualifications, others by department or funding stream.

Whether the team meetings are for quality improvement or internal quality assurance purposes, the agenda should start with the following key points:

- who is present or who is absent and why
- confirmation that the minutes from the last meeting are a true and accurate record
- an update regarding any actions or matters arising from the previous meeting (a record will have been issued to everyone in the form of *minutes*).

A quality improvement or internal quality assurance meeting will usually include topics for discussion such as:

- recruitment, new starters and leavers
- retention and attendance

- pass rates
- tracking of learner progress including reviews
- learners at risk
- learner voice activities and feedback (including questionnaires and survey results)
- employer surveys and feedback
- equality and diversity
- safeguarding and prevent duty
- health and safety
- maths and English (functional skills)
- training needs and continuing personal development activities
- any changes or updates to standards and/or qualifications
- any other business.

A quality improvement meeting often also includes:

- progress made towards the quality improvement plan (QIP)
- information, advice and guidance (IAG) and careers development (Gatsby benchmarks – see Appendix 4)
- quality improvement activities (deep dives – see the Introduction Chapter)
- feedback from any internal or external inspections
- learner and employer feedback from relevant forums
- complaints.

An internal quality assurance meeting will also include:

- programme: changes or updates to standards and/or qualifications
- developing employability skills
- assessment: types and methods used, issues or concerns
- internal quality assurance (IQA): observations and sampling dates, registrations and certification, appeals and complaints, general feedback to assessors from IQA monitoring activities
- external quality assurance: feedback and reports, action plans, updates from awarding organisations
- standardisation: feedback from recent activities, planning new activities and dates.

You might chair the meeting yourself or someone else in your organisation might do it. Someone will need to be responsible for accurately taking the minutes of the meeting. After the meeting, the minutes and any actions should be circulated to the whole team. Actions should have target dates, and the name of the person who will carry them out.

Team meetings can be held face to face or through electronic media or a platform which enables group video calling for remote access.

# What can it be used for?

Team meetings are a great way to bring everyone involved in the learner journey together. They are an open opportunity to reflect on progress, celebrate achievement, identify any issues or concerns, and to put actions in place to improve general performance.

The minutes of the meetings are an official record of the actions taken at the meeting which are used to inform attendees and non-attendees of what was discussed or what happened during the meeting. They can also be used as evidence of addressing any mandatory requirements for awarding organisations, statutory and regulatory visits, audits and inspections. For example, standardisation activities are a mandatory requirement of offering a regulated qualification via an awarding organisation.

# Resources

- A physical or virtual environment to hold the meeting
- A method of documenting the minutes, i.e. visual, aural, digitally recorded, or manually documented

# Advantages

👍 Enables the team members to problem solve together and voice their opinions or concerns

👍 Supports team members' morale if everyone is included

👍 Creates an official record of what was discussed or happened

👍 Can be used as evidence of a mandatory activity taking place

# Disadvantages

👎 Can be time-consuming

👎 Can be dominated by some individuals and others might digress

👎 Not all team members may take it seriously

---

### Tip

If you are chairing the meeting, ask a colleague to take notes of what was discussed and produce the minutes afterwards. This will enable you to focus on what's happening in the meeting rather than trying to chair the discussions and take notes.

# Further reading and weblinks

Beardwell I & Holden L (1997) *Human Resource Management*. London: Pitman Publishing.

Crawshaw J et al. (2014) *Human Resource Management*. London: SAGE Publications.

Gravells A (2016) *Principles and Practices of Quality Assurance*. London: Learning Matters.

KLSTraining – *Tips for chairing meetings* – https://tinyurl.com/y93baexe

# 26 Managing unsatisfactory performance

| IQA activity | √ | EQA activity | √ | Deep dive activity | |
| In person | √ | Remote | √ | Electronic/online | |
| Includes learners | | Includes assessors | | Includes others | √ |
| Promotes standardisation | | Lead IQA role | √ | Quality improvement role | √ |

## What is it?

Managing unsatisfactory performance is about knowing what to do when a member of your team has not performed their role correctly. You can be either proactive, i.e. respond to a situation before it becomes serious, or reactive by dealing with it once it has.

Unsatisfactory performance could be due to many reasons, personal or professional. This could be an individual's fault, e.g. not being honest with regard to their knowledge when they applied for the position. Or it could be the fault of the organisation by not conveying crucial information, e.g. when a policy has changed. Recruiting, inducting and retaining staff (see Chapter 18) who have the necessary skills, knowledge and experience will hopefully keep staff turnover low. If the organisation invests in training and ongoing support for their team members, this should enable them to carry out their job role effectively. However, there may be times when an individual does not perform satisfactorily, and this will need to be dealt with.

## What can it be used for?

It can be used to support staff to improve their performance, or to understand what they have done wrong with a view to putting it right.

There should be a policy within your organisation for dealing with unsatisfactory performance, which might lead to disciplinary action if an individual does not conform. For example, if an individual's performance is not up to standard, an informal discussion could take place first to establish the reasons, and to agree any necessary action. If the action cannot be reasonably achieved due to individual circumstances, the staff member should be given the opportunity for support, such as further training or assistance. In more serious circumstances, and following the correct procedure, they could be offered a reduction in their workload, some counselling or stress management.

Disciplinary action could occur if the individual's performance constitutes misconduct. There will be organisational procedures to follow and the process might be linked to performance appraisals (see Chapter 23). Formal records should always be maintained and relevant employment law followed.

Hopefully, your staff member will improve, make progress and meet the standards required. If you don't want the situation to escalate through the disciplinary procedure process, you might be able to offer them a different job role or look at reducing their workload or hours. There are many reasons why someone might not be performing well and these should all be taken into consideration. You will need to liaise with relevant personnel in your organisation, such as those from the human resources department, to ensure any contracts and/or terms of employment/equality legislation have not been breached.

Unsatisfactory performance of an individual could reflect badly on you and your organisation. It is therefore important to identify any issues quickly, discover the causes, and put an action plan in place to rectify them. If staff members are not performing adequately, there may be an impact upon others and the reputation of the organisation.

## Resources

- Records such as appraisals and performance reviews
- Action plan template

## Advantages

👍 Enables you to support and train staff as necessary

## Disadvantages

👎 Staff might not be aware they are doing something wrong, perhaps if they have not been adequately trained or inducted

---

### Tip

You may find it useful to mentor your team members or pair them up to provide mutual support to each other. You could also create a culture of openness to enable staff to talk to you in confidence, perhaps if they identify another staff member is not performing satisfactorily.

---

# Further reading and weblinks

Adair J (2002) *John Adair's 100 Greatest Ideas for Effective Leadership and Management.* Mankato: Capstone.

Personnel Today – *Managing poor performance at work* – https://tinyurl.com/ybphd44m

Wallace S and Gravells J (2007) *Leadership and Leading Teams.* Exeter: Learning Matters.

Wallace S and Gravells J (2007) *Mentoring in the Lifelong Learning Sector.* Exeter: Learning Matters.

# 27 Observing staff and using learning walks

| IQA activity | √ | EQA activity | √ | Deep dive activity | √ |
|---|---|---|---|---|---|
| In person | √ | Remote | √ | Electronic/online | √ |
| Includes learners | √ | Includes assessors | √ | Includes others | √ |
| Promotes standardisation | √ | Lead IQA role | √ | Quality improvement role | √ |

## What is it?

Observations are about watching a member of staff deliver a section of their session to their learners as part of a quality improvement role. Alternatively, it can be part of a quality assurance activity carried out by an internal quality assurer (IQA) watching an assessor make an assessment decision regarding a learner's performance.

A learning walk is a type of observation which enables the observer to capture a *snapshot* of what is happening during the session. It can take place at the start, middle or end of the session, and usually lasts between 10 to 15 minutes. Some organisations choose to have learning walk *themes* which they share with staff. For example; embedding applied maths or English into a practical session in preparation for employment, or learning activities which have a focus on diversity. The observer would check to see if what is taking place has been planned around the *theme*.

Observations generally last between 15 and 60 minutes. However, they can be longer, for example; to observe a full session from beginning to end. They could also be visually recorded (with the permission of all those involved). This would enable staff to view the recording later, either on their own or with their peers, to evaluate the process and discuss possible improvements. The observer or IQA should follow set criteria which all staff are familiar with, to ensure a standardised approach.

Observations which are used for quality improvement can be graded or ungraded depending on what you are using them for, and the needs of your organisation. Although very rarely used now to judge an individual session, an example of the grades that could be used are:

- grade one – outstanding
- grade two – good
- grade three – requires improvement
- grade four – inadequate.

Whether you are grading or not, the whole purpose of an observation is to provide feedback to the member of staff as to how they can further improve their practice. That feedback should also include a discussion about what went well, why it went well and how the member of staff can maintain or build upon the positives. If an external inspector or quality assurer is carrying out an observation, the member of staff might not receive individual feedback. This is because the findings will form part of an overall judgement using other evidence from the organisation, such as a range of observations and learner interviews.

When using an observation as part of a quality assurance activity, for example; to see the assessment process carried out with a learner, the IQA should agree when and where the observation will take place. This will ensure a direct observation of the assessment practice, i.e. the learner carrying out one or more tasks, the assessment decision and the subsequent feedback.

# What can it be used for?

Observations are a great way to assess the skills, knowledge and attitudes of a member of staff, that they are teaching in a manner that ensures learning is taking place, that learners are making good or better progress over time, and to be assured that the correct assessment decisions are being made. Observations can be carried out solely by the IQA or as part of a quality improvement role, or they can be a paired activity with another observer, to support standardisation.

A learning walk should be used as part of a deep dive activity (see the Introduction Chapter) and not as a measure of the member of staff's performance on its own. For example, if learners are undertaking a task, you could ask them some questions about what they are doing and why they are doing it. This will help you to put into context what you are observing, however you should only speak to the learners if an appropriate opportunity arises.

Observations can be used in an informal supportive manner to improve an individual's confidence and performance, or as a formative measure where the observer's findings are documented and used for a specific purpose.

If a member of staff is found to not be performing to the required criteria, an action plan should be agreed and developed identifying what support will be available and what training they must undertake. The action plan could include the member of staff observing others who do meet the criteria, providing them with a mentor, and informal observations with constructive feedback. A date should be arranged for a formal re-observation after the member of staff has completed all the actions. If the member of staff fails to improve their performance, the organisation may decide to take formal action, for example; by following the relevant procedure.

Anyone working towards an initial teacher training or assessment qualification might also be observed as part of the qualification criteria.

# Resources

- Set criteria or an observation checklist (records must be maintained)
- Action plan template

# Advantages

- Supports standardisation
- Can improve performance if feedback is given skillfully
- Gives some assurance that what should be happening is happening

# Disadvantages

- The member of staff may be anxious about being observed and their performance may suffer
- The learners' behaviour might change
- The observer might be biased with their judgement

> **Tip**
>
> If you are using observation as part of a quality improvement role, do not give the member of staff any notice that you are going to observe them. Carrying out unannounced observations puts less stress on the member of staff in terms of the anxiety of planning their session, as they know observations could happen at any time.

# Further reading and weblinks

The Classroom – *Advantages and disadvantages of using observation for teacher evaluation* – https://tinyurl.com/uq7tyv2

# 28 Planning and tracking internal quality assurance activities

| IQA activity | √ | EQA activity | | Deep dive activity | |
|---|---|---|---|---|---|
| In person | | Remote | √ | Electronic/online | √ |
| Includes learners | | Includes assessors | | Includes others | * |
| Promotes standardisation | √ | Lead IQA role | * | Quality improvement role | * |

*depends upon what and how you are planning to use the approach*

## What is it?

Planning and tracking internal quality assurance activities is part of the job role of an internal quality assurer (IQA). It is a requirement if your organisation offers qualifications which are accredited via an awarding organisation (AO). Records must be maintained of all aspects relating to internal quality assurance for auditing and inspection purposes. You could use a template for your planning and tracking, i.e. as a hard copy or in electronic form. A completed example is available in Appendix 1.

The planning aspect will be based on your IQA rationale (see Chapter 15) and sampling strategy (see Chapter 16). Planning involves deciding what will be sampled, from whom and when, and the activities will be based on any identified risks (see Chapter 24). The awarding organisation might prescribe the number of learners which must be sampled. If you are quality assuring a non-accredited qualification, or the awarding organisation does not prescribe what should be sampled, then you should (as a minimum) consider the following points to decide the size of a sample to undertake:

- all assessors must be sampled across all units, but new or inexperienced assessors should be sampled more frequently to ensure they are assessing correctly

- a qualification which is being delivered for the first time should be sampled more frequently to ensure standardisation of practice by all assessors, and identify any issues or trends

- If the qualification is broken down into modules or units, each one should be sampled across the majority of learners

- any special considerations a learner may have been awarded. (For example; if a learner has been awarded extra time, then they should be sampled in the same way as all other learners).

The tracking aspect will document what was sampled, from whom and when, and be backed up with supporting records of your findings (see Chapter 21). Don't worry if the dates on your tracking sheet don't match exactly with those on your plan. This is normal as circumstances do change. For example; you might have planned to observe an assessor carrying out an activity with their learner on a certain day, but the learner goes on holiday.

# What can it be used for?

Planning and tracking can be used to ensure that:

- your assessors are performing their job role correctly
- you support the development of your staff team
- you know what has been done and when
- you meet AO requirements.

As a minimum, you will need:

- an observation plan
- a meeting and standardisation plan
- a sample plan and tracking sheet.

You could have separate plans for each activity if there are a lot of assessors and learners, or combine them if numbers are small.

The plans will identify who you will observe and when, when meetings and standardisation activities will take place, and what you will sample from each assessor and when. They should show that there will be continual activity over the period of assessment for a particular qualification or programme of learning. However, you can deviate from your plans when necessary. For example; if you identify a particular assessor has misinterpreted some criteria, you may want to sample the same criteria from other assessors to see if there is a trend.

To decide on what to sample, you should consider the following:

- assessors: qualifications, experience, workload, caseload, locations
- learners: any particular requirements, ethnic origin, age, gender, locations
- qualification content: units which could be misinterpreted or which contain complex assessment criteria
- methods of assessment: observation, questions, tests, simulation, prior learning
- learners' evidence: documents, work products, responses to questions, assignments, witness testimonies, visual recordings
- records and decisions: assessment planning and feedback records; validity and reliability of assessment methods and judgements.

There are various sampling methods you could use; some are more effective than others. The following terminology relates to how they are viewed on a sample plan, for example:

- diagonal (a different aspect from all learners)
- horizontal (different aspects from the same learner over time)
- vertical (the same aspect from different learners)
- percentage (e.g. 10 per cent from each assessor or learner, however this is not good practice as aspects can easily be missed)
- random (unsystematic method but useful as an additional sample if an issue is found)
- theme based (relating to a particular area of assessment such as work products, questions or witness testimonies).

A mixture of diagonal, horizontal and vertical sampling is best as it ensures everything will be monitored over time, as in Appendix 1. If IQA is carried out towards or at the end of the assessment process, there is little opportunity to rectify any concerns or issues.

The IQA should create the sampling plan as soon as learners are enrolled, and/or registered for a qualification with an awarding organisation. It should include all units or modules, and all types, methods and activities of the assessment methods used. Whichever methods you use, they should be fit for purpose and ensure that something from each assessor is sampled over time. You are looking for quality, not quantity, and you can look at work in progress (formative) and work completed (summative).

The actual date of your samples can be added to your tracking sheet to show an audit trail from planning to completion. You can analyse what has taken place in order to revise your IQA rationale and sampling strategy. You can also provide a summary of your findings to your assessors to aid the standardisation of practice, to share findings of good practice, and to clarify any misunderstandings.

## Resources

- A method of planning the sample such as an electronic calendar
- A method of tracking the sample, which could be the same document as the plan
- Templates to record the findings from the activities undertaken

## Advantages

- Maintains compliance with AO requirements
- Ensures staff are performing as they should
- Helps to identify good and bad practice

# Disadvantages

👎 Can be time-consuming to plan all the different activities

👎 Staff might change and learners might leave, therefore the plan needs continual updating

---

### Tip

You can gain valuable feedback from learners and witnesses if you factor dates for discussions with them into your plan.

---

# Further reading and weblinks

Gravells A (2016) *Principles and Practices of Quality Assurance*. London: Learning Matters.

Pontin K (2012) *Practical Guide to Quality Assurance*. London: City & Guilds.

Read H (2012) *The Best Quality Assurer's Guide*. Bideford: Read On Publications.

Wilson L (2012) *Practical Teaching: A Guide to Assessment and Quality Assurance*. Andover: Cengage Learning.

# 29 Planning and tracking quality improvement activities

| IQA activity | √ | EQA activity | * | Deep dive activity | √ |
|---|---|---|---|---|---|
| In person | √ | Remote | * | Electronic/online | * |
| Includes learners | | Includes assessors | √ | Includes others | √ |
| Promotes standardisation | √ | Lead IQA role | * | Quality improvement role | √ |

*depends upon what and how you are planning to use the approach*

## What is it?

It's important to plan and track the quality improvement activities you will carry out, to ensure that they are fit for purpose, that records are maintained for audit purposes, and that relevant targets are achieved.

The activities can be based on the organisation's strategic aims (see Chapter 30) and key performance indicators (KPIs) which detail how the aims will be met, by whom and by when.

KPI's could include targets for:

- a curriculum that reflects local needs
- minimum required attendance
- retention rates
- pass rates
- positive destinations
- growth and finances
- employer engagement
- English and maths achievement
- information, advice and guidance
- staff training, qualifications to be achieved, and continuing professional development activities
- compliance towards audit processes of external inspectorates, awarding organisations and other agencies.

In addition, to the KPIs which need to be achieved, there should also be a quality improvement plan (QIP) which is developed from the previous year's self-assessment report (SAR) (see Chapter 50), along with action points.

For example, a general further education college identified in their SAR that: *English and mathematics teachers do not routinely use the information from assessment to inform their teaching. As a result, too many learners are unclear how teaching builds on their existing knowledge.*

One of the college's strategic aims is therefore: *To ensure all learners attain a minimum requirement of English and maths and that all programmes provide the opportunity for English and maths enhancement.* The college identify in their QIP that they are introducing a new assessment tool which provides information for leaders and teachers about how teaching should address gaps in knowledge. As part of the quality improvement activities, the organisation will need to plan regular dates to monitor and measure the impact regarding how the new assessment tool impacts on learning and if it is having the desired results.

The quality improvement activities could include:

- checking schemes of work or that session plans have effective links to English and maths
- the quality manager undertaking learning walks (see Chapter 27)
- learner and teacher interviews (see Chapter 43)
- questionnaires and surveys (see Chapter 14)
- tracking of learner data over a number of months, to measure if the new assessment tool has a positive impact on learning, and if learners are attaining at least the minimum requirements.

Each activity must be tracked and evidence such as reports and data collated to support the college to measure the progress towards their KPIs and QIP action points.

Alternatively, you could decide to focus on developing a strength further, or you might have a lack of evidence towards a particular strategic aim and decide to plan and track quality improvement activities based around it.

For example, a strategic aim based on the quality of education at a private training organisation is to: *Develop and implement a vibrant, relevant and attractive curriculum, meeting local and regional skills' needs and priorities.*

The quality improvement activities could include:

- research of the local and regional skills' needs in relation to the curriculum offered (including the Local Enterprise Partnership (LEP), local authority and employers) mapped across the curriculum offered
- employer engagement in relation to courses offered
- checking schemes of work and session plans for links to the local area's needs and requirements
- obtaining learner feedback through questionnaires and/or surveys in relation to their career aspirations
- achievement and destination data.

# What can it be used for?

Quality improvement activities can be used to improve performance across your organisation.

Planning regular dates for activities which monitor the progress towards your organisation's KPIs and/or action points from your QIP will support progress. By tracking each activity you are ensuring it has taken place, and are able to scrutinise the evidence to ensure everything is progressing in the direction you require.

You may need to increase your plan regarding the monitoring activities if you identify through your tracking that you are not achieving the desired progress. Equally you may decide to decrease your plan if you are making rapid progress.

# Resources

• A method of planning and tracking the quality improvement activities such as an electronic calendar

• Templates to document the evidence from the quality improvement activities undertaken

# Advantages

👍 Helps staff to understand the expectations of the organisation

👍 Gives measurable results

👍 Supports standardisation

# Disadvantages

👎 Implementing changes to improve quality can be costly at the start

👎 If the KPIs and the QIP are not explained well to staff, this can discourage creativity and innovation

👎 Can cause staff to become too focused on results and lose motivation on the quality of other areas

---

Tip

To support you to manage the quality improvement activities, it is helpful to develop a quality improvement calendar. This shows all planned dates and activities that will be undertaken throughout the year towards the KPIs and the QIP.

# Further reading and weblinks

Education and Training Foundation Excellence Gateway – https://tinyurl.com/rxd3gzh

Education and Training Foundation Quality Improvement Toolkit for Education and Training Providers – https://tinyurl.com/y7ddtmx9

# 30 Planning strategic aims and continuous quality improvement

| IQA activity | √ | EQA activity | | Deep dive activity | |
|---|---|---|---|---|---|
| In person | √ | Remote | * | Electronic/online | * |
| Includes learners | √ | Includes assessors | √ | Includes others | √ |
| Promotes standardisation | √ | Lead IQA role | * | Quality improvement role | √ |

*depends upon what and how you are planning to use the approach*

## What is it?

Organisations offering education and training provision must be committed to continuous quality improvement, to improve the learning experience for all concerned. This usually starts with your organisation's strategic aims which reflect its vision, mission and values. These are usually displayed on your organisation's website.

For example:

An independent training provider offering beauty therapy and related courses aims to:

*Create an organisational culture which is responsive, effective and dynamic in a world of change. It will value staff, providing best possible conditions of service, sustainable jobs, career development and progression.*

Their strategic aims are to:

- *engage and progress more people into higher levels of learning and/or employment, supporting aspirations and ensuring a positive destination for every learner*
- *provide a safe and outstanding learning experience for all*
- *develop the capability and capacity of our staff to contribute effectively to quality, enterprise, sustainable development, and innovation of the curriculum*
- *ensure strong financial health, and organisational sustainability from effective use of our staff and resources.*

Their strategic aims are further described by stating expectations:

We are an organisation:

- *where learners come first, feel safe and where the curriculum meets the needs of the local and wider economy and there is a continuing commitment to high academic standards and excellence in learning, teaching and assessment*

- *in which there is straightforward, two-way communication that is consistent, respectful and honest with united and skilled staff*

- *recognised as a provider of choice for learners and employers*

- *which provides relevant and inclusive provision accessible to all learners and which allows for individual pathways supported by high quality information, advice and guidance*

- *where every member of staff takes responsibility for quality*

- *which continuously strives for excellence.*

Having comprehensive strategic aims will contribute towards continuous quality improvement within the organisation.


# What can it be used for?

To achieve the strategic aims and to ensure continuous quality improvement within the organisation, all staff should have certain responsibilities, for example:

Senior managers:

- contributing to strategic planning and raising standards by improving achievement rates

- promoting quality awareness with all staff

- developing procedures through which to evaluate the effectiveness of learning

- developing a range of qualitative and quantitative indicators through which efficiency and effectiveness can be monitored and evaluated

- offering support and training in areas of weakness to improve practice

- providing information, advice and guidance regarding all aspects of quality

- reporting on assessment of the quality of staff performance

- preparing and supporting staff in responding to the review and audit processes of external inspectorates, awarding organisations and other agencies

- ensuring that all policies and procedures are adhered to and embedded across the provision offered.

Managers:

- identifying the strategic priorities for their department in response to internal and external demands and initiatives

- planning and co-ordinating information, advice and guidance activities and ensuring staff are trained and working to the Matrix Standards and Gatsby Benchmarks (see Appendix 4).

- agreeing targets for teaching and learning, and communicating them to staff

- managing the quality cycle in their area
- reviewing all improvement plans
- collating and acting on feedback from learners, employers and other stakeholders including compliments and complaints
- monitoring compliance with quality issues
- overseeing staff performance in their area, ensuring appropriate inductions and relevant training.

Senior teachers:

- ensuring that all members of the delivery team (teaching and support), comply with current requirements of the course and are aware of the performance targets such as attendance, retention and pass rates, targets for progression and growth
- ensuring that monitoring of performance targets and quality improvement occurs through regular team meetings
- ensuring that results of performance measurements are reported to management, and that action planning takes place to use these results to positively effect quality improvement
- ensuring that all policies and procedures are adhered to and embedded across the provision
- producing a team development plan agreeing targets to maintain strengths, address areas of concern and quality improvements.

Teachers:

- reviewing the learner journey including attendance and achievement
- reviewing induction, teaching, learning, assessment and quality assurance activities
- reviewing learner and employer feedback and responding appropriately
- following all policies and procedures
- reviewing progress towards targets during course meetings throughout the year
- providing effective and appropriate teaching, and support for learning
- maintaining course files and ensuring adherence to teaching, learning and assessment requirements, participating in internal and external reviews, observation and performance systems, undertaking appropriate development and training with the intention of driving up standards.

Administrative staff:

- ensuring that the quality of service to internal and external customers is compliant with organisational requirements
- ensuring that staff are supported and assisted in the achievement of their quality objectives
- ensuring that monitoring and evaluation of all products and services takes place at regular team meetings, and that action planning is used to positively affect quality improvements

- following all policies and procedures
- undertaking appropriate development and training with the intention of driving up standards
- supporting recruitment and retention activities by providing information, advice and guidance which are consistent and within the limits of the member of staff's knowledge and expertise, signposting individuals to a manager as appropriate.

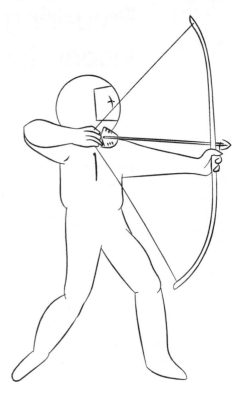

## Resources

- A method of documenting the evidence from the activities undertaken

## Advantages

👍 Helps to assure a better quality of performance in every sphere of activity

👍 Promotes standardisation and embeds a culture of high quality

## Disadvantages

👎 Can make staff anxious and fearful for their jobs if activities are not communicated well

👎 Implementing changes to improve quality can be costly at the start

> **Tip**
>
> Organisations who focus on continuously raising standards when performance targets are reached, and who frequently review their strategic aims, can perform better than those who don't.

## Further reading and weblinks

AOC – *Quality Improvement and Regulations* – https://tinyurl.com/ydhor9r8

Education and Training Foundation – *Quality Improvement Toolkit for Education and Training Providers* – https://tinyurl.com/y7ddtmx9

# 31 Preparing for an external inspection

| IQA | √ | EQA | | Deep dive activity | √ |
|---|---|---|---|---|---|
| In person | √ | Remote | √ | Electronic/online | √ |
| Includes learners | √ | Includes assessors | √ | Includes others | √ |
| Promotes standardisation | √ | Lead IQA role | | Quality improvement role | √ |

## What is it?

There are a number of external inspections which a quality practitioner may experience, e.g. from the Care Quality Commission (CQC), Independent Schools Council (ISC), the Quality Improvement Agency (QIA) and/or the Quality Assurance Agency (QAA). However, this chapter will consider the inspection process which you are most likely to experience which will be from Ofsted.

*The Office for Standards in Education, Children's Services and Skills (Ofsted) regulates and inspects to achieve excellence in the care of children and young people, and in education and skills for learners of all ages. It regulates and inspects childcare and children's social care, and inspects the Children and Family Court Advisory and Support Service (Cafcass), schools, colleges, initial teacher training, further education and skills, adult and community learning, and education and training in prisons and other secure establishments. It assesses council children's services, and inspects services for children looked after, safeguarding and child protection.* (https://tinyurl.com/y9c742fm).

If your organisation receives government funding and is included in the above, you will be inspected at some point. The different types of inspection undertaken by Ofsted include:

- full inspection
- short inspection
- survey and research visits
- monitoring visits
- monitoring visits to providers that are newly directly funded.

For a full inspection Ofsted use a range of principles to inspect providers which includes an evaluation schedule, the education and inspection framework (EIF), a four-point scale and grade descriptors.

Inspectors will use the following four-point scale to make judgements based on the information they gather during the inspection:

- Grade 1 – the provision is outstanding
- Grade 2 – the provision is at least good
- Grade 3 – the provision requires improvement
- Grade 4 – the provision is inadequate.

During the inspection, judgements are made regarding overall effectiveness and the four key judgements of:

- the quality of education
- behaviour and attitudes
- personal development
- leadership and management.

As part of their judgement, inspectors will also consider if safeguarding arrangements are appropriate and effective. On the final day of inspection, they will consider the evidence and grades used for the four key judgments and give an overall effectiveness grade.

Generally, if a provider receives a good or better grade for overall effectiveness, Ofsted will undertake a short inspection rather than a full inspection within five years (an outstanding provider is not usually subject to any routine inspection). If a provider is deemed as requiring improvement they will receive a monitoring visit within seven to 13 months and normally be fully inspected within 12 to 30 months. Providers who are judged inadequate will receive a number of monitoring visits before being re-inspected within 13 months.

Of the four key judgements, much of the evidence will be gathered through *the quality of education* criteria, which are divided into three areas, i.e. intent, implementation and impact.

The maximum time your organisation will have to prepare for an Ofsted inspection is two working days, although it is not unusual to have no notice. Ofsted staff will notify the principal (or equivalent) of the inspection date via a telephone call. This is followed shortly after with an email confirming the dates of inspection (a full inspection is usually carried out over four days, a short inspection over two days) and requesting a telephone planning meeting with the provider's nominee, usually on the same day. The nominee will be asked to upload any evidence they feel is appropriate to the inspection, to the Ofsted portal. This usually includes the provider's self-assessment report, timetables and confirmation of on-programme learner numbers, the courses, and locations of where they are undertaken. The lead inspector will use the information which has been uploaded to decide how best to place their team inspectors. The number of inspectors will depend on the size of the organisation. The nominee should inform all staff of the inspection and ask them to have learning materials and documentation available for scrutiny when the inspectors visit their classes, or speak to them or their learners.

## What can it be used for?

It can be used to ensure that your organisational culture is one of quality improvement with clear quality assurance processes, and that all staff know and understand what they are.

Using the EIF as a basis of your quality improvement planning will ensure you are prepared well before you receive a notification of inspection. To check your organisation is inspection ready you should be able to connect different sources of good practice to triangulate evidence. For example, you may undertake an observation of a taught session in a workshop and see learners demonstrating high level skills. You could follow this up by interviewing a small group of learners to find out how they will use the skills in the workplace or progress to the next level of education or work. This could be followed up by checking past learner destination data, and a few phone calls to previous learners to check if they are still in related employment.

Here is an example of how you could check and triangulate the three areas of intent, implementation and impact for the quality of education (often called a deep dive – see the Introduction Chapter):

- Intent – discussions with senior and subject teachers to identify the reasons for the choice of curriculum and what the intended progression for the learners is. How the content will be taught in a logical sequence, methodically and explicitly for all learners to obtain the intended knowledge, skills and behaviours. Other evidence could include employer and learner feedback which supports the curriculum offered.

- Implementation – discussions with teachers about how they are supported to address their own knowledge gaps. Details of the curriculum which their learners are following including the sequencing of learning, why a particular topic is being delivered at a particular stage and how prior knowledge and skills are being incorporated into delivery. The intended end point, and the teachers' view on how the learners are progressing so far. Learning walks, observations of teaching (see Chapter 27), and discussions or interviews with learners including ascertaining whether they feel safe. Following selected learners through their learning journey including the application and enrolment process, initial assessment and subsequent tutorial reviews which demonstrate progress towards the individual's targets or aspirations. Scrutiny of work produced by learners and the feedback they have received. This may include joint work scrutiny (see Chapter 43).

- Impact – discussions (these may be by telephone) with a selection of learners about their destinations. Nationally generated and validated performance information about learner progress and attainment. Information gathered under implementation (above) may also be used.

Using this example could also support you to understand how well your organisation is performing regarding aspects of learners' behaviour and attitudes. You could consider the following points to help you:

- is learning taking place in a safe, calm and orderly environment?
- how good is attendance and punctuality?
- are learners well behaved, respectful, motivated and do they have positive attitudes?
- do staff deal with any issues quickly, consistently and effectively?

In addition, the example picks up on personal development if you consider the following points:

- are learners developing their confidence and resilience which goes beyond the curriculum?

- are teachers promoting equality of opportunity to enable all learners to flourish together?

- is there effective career advice to help learners make good choices and understand what they need to do to reach their aspirations?

The art of preparing for an external inspection is by ensuring well in advance that all staff understand the criteria of good quality education. The *Ofsted Further Education and Skills Inspection Handbook* (2020) describes the main activities that inspectors will carry out. Part one contains information about the process of inspection before during and afterwards. Part two contains the evaluation schedule which will help you to put your own processes and practices in place prior to the inspection.

## Resources

- Depends on how you are using the approach
- *Ofsted Further Education and Skills Inspection Handbook* (2020)

## Advantages

👍 Helps embed a positive culture

👍 Can be less stressful if you are well organised when Ofsted inspectors arrive

## Disadvantages

👎 Not all staff are willing to change the way they have always done things

👎 Some key staff might not be available during the inspection

---

### Tip

Try to have a positive culture which is always proactive, and operates as though an inspection could take place at any time. It's better to have high standards to be the norm, rather than panicking to try and achieve them when notified of an inspection date.

Ofsted often update their handbook, so always check for the latest version which might include changes affecting the content of this chapter.

## Further reading and weblinks

For Schools Education Services – *The new Ofsted Criteria and Work Scrutiny* – https://tinyurl.com/wlq4jea

Ofsted – *Further Education and Skills Inspection Handbook* (2020) – https://tinyurl.com/y9kn8gxk

# 32 Preparing for an external quality assurance remote sample

| IQA activity | √ | EQA activity | | Deep dive activity | * |
|---|---|---|---|---|---|
| In person | | Remote | √ | Electronic/online | √ |
| Includes learners | * | Includes assessors | √ | Includes others | * |
| Promotes standardisation | | Lead IQA role | √ | Quality improvement role | * |

*depends upon what and how you are planning to use the approach*

## What is it?

Preparing for an external quality assurance (EQA) remote sample will be a requirement if your organisation offers accredited or endorsed qualifications through an awarding organisation (AO). It might occur if you have small numbers of learners, or the previous EQA visits resulted in *low* or *no* action points. An EQA remote sample can also be used by the AO for a generic activity such as reviewing policies and procedures.

The EQA or a representative from the AO will make contact to arrange a suitable date for the remote sample to take place. You will be required to post, email or give remote electronic access to learners' work, along with the requested documents and records. This might include:

- a list of trainers, assessors and IQAs, with evidence of their continuing professional development (CPD)
- CVs of any new staff along with copies of their certificates
- copies of minutes of meetings and records of standardisation activities
- details of learners, their locations and registration and/or unit completion and certification dates
- learner evidence, supporting assessment and feedback records
- internal quality assurance (IQA) tracking, sampling and feedback records
- evidence of meeting any previous action points which may include confirmation of reviewing and/or updating policies and procedures.

If you are allowing access to documents, records or evidence by remote means, you must follow the general data protection regulations (GDPR).

The EQA might ask to speak to certain learners, staff and expert witnesses at set times during the sample day. If so, you will need to supply relevant telephone numbers and ensure that those individuals are aware they will be called.

# What can it be used for?

An EQA remote sample can be carried out instead of a visit where a centre is performing well, and/or has low numbers of learners, or is subject to a lockdown.

You should involve your team members to prepare the requested items for the remote sample. Always refer to any previous EQA reports to ensure all action points have been met, as you will need to provide evidence of this. If any have not been met, you might be given a sanction. This means that certification rights could be removed until the issues are resolved.

If electronic access is to be given to the EQA, you will need to liaise with relevant personnel in your organisation. This might involve creating a one-time password and ensuring access can be gained on the day.

When the EQA has completed their sample, they might telephone you to discuss their findings. However, sometimes due to time constraints, an EQA may submit the report straight to the AO without speaking to you. Generally they will discuss and agree any action and improvement points with you, and inform you of how and when you can access a copy of their report. Make sure you discuss the report with your team afterwards, and that you complete any action points by the agreed dates.

The AO or EQA will return any items which have been received by them. Make sure they have the right name, department, and full address for them to return these.

# Resources

- Previous EQA report
- Evidence of meeting any action points from the previous EQA report
- All documents, learner evidence and records requested by the EQA
- The address of the AO or EQA to post the requested items
- Remote access to any electronic learners' work and supporting records (if applicable)

# Advantages

- Should take up less time than a visit
- Certificates could be issued in a faster time frame from a remote sample than a face-to-face visit (the latter sometimes only taking place once or twice a year)

# Disadvantages

👎 Relies on other staff getting the information and documentation to you in advance, and being available at a set time if the EQA wants to talk to them

👎 Arranging a courier or packaging and taking items to the post office can be time-consuming and expensive

👎 Items might be delayed or lost in the post

👎 If the EQA is accessing learner evidence and records remotely, there might be problems gaining access to your system on the day

👎 The EQA might have to telephone you several times if things are not self-explanatory, or if you have not provided everything they have requested

---

### Tip

If you don't have something which has been requested, inform the EQA of the reason why, well in advance. This gives them the opportunity to request something else instead. Don't just substitute an alternative as this will highlight a risk. The EQA might feel you've made a substitution to hide something.

---

# Further reading and weblinks

Gravells A (2016) *Principles and Practices of Quality Assurance*. London: Learning Matters.

Pontin K (2012) *Practical Guide to Quality Assurance*. London: City & Guilds.

Read H (2011) *The Best Internal Quality Assurer's Guide*. Bideford: Read On Publications.

# 33 Preparing for an external quality assurance visit

| IQA activity | √ | EQA activity | | Deep dive activity | * |
|---|---|---|---|---|---|
| In person | √ | Remote | | Electronic/online | |
| Includes learners | √ | Includes assessors | √ | Includes others | * |
| Promotes standardisation | √ | Lead IQA role | √ | Quality improvement role | √ |

*depends upon what and how you are planning to use the approach

## What is it?

Preparing for an external quality assurance (EQA) visit will be a requirement if your organisation offers qualifications through an awarding organisation (AO). At some point, an external quality assurer from the AO will visit to ensure compliance with their requirements.

How often these visits take place, their duration and the activities carried out, will depend upon the requirements of the qualification and how active your organisation is. The EQA or a representative from the AO will make contact to arrange a suitable date and time for the visit. They will have documentation which they will send to you outlining the information they will require prior to the visit. This might include:

- a list of teachers, trainers, assessors, witnesses, IQAs and their locations
- evidence of staff undertaking continuing professional development (CPD) (see Chapter 7), copies of staff CVs and the original certificates which qualify them to undertake their role
- copies of minutes of meetings and records of standardisation activities
- details of learners, their locations and registration and/or unit completion and certification dates
- evidence of centre policies and procedures which have been reviewed and/or updated.

The AO or EQA will use this information to plan what they want to see and from whom. They will be able to compare your learners' names and registration/certification dates with those on the AOs database. If any information is different, this will highlight an anomaly for them to check with you.

Once the AO or EQA has the relevant information, they will send you a *visit and sample plan*. This will state what they will want to achieve during their visit and who they will want to see. This might include:

- looking at assessment, internal quality assurance (IQA) and other supporting documents and records such as policies and procedures

- meeting the team

- observing assessor and IQA practice

- reviewing feedback from learners

- reviewing staff members' CPD activities

- sampling learners' work and supporting assessment records

- talking to learners and witnesses.

If you don't have something which has been requested, inform the EQA of the reason why, well in advance. This gives them the opportunity to request something else instead. Don't just substitute an alternative as this will highlight a risk. The EQA might feel you've made a substitution to hide something.

You should involve your team members when preparing for the visit, and refer to any previous EQA reports to ensure all action points have been met. If any have not been met, you might be given a sanction. This means that certification rights could be removed until the issues are resolved.

# What can it be used for?

Preparing for an EQA visit can ensure that you and your team are well organised for the activities which will be carried out on the day.

You might like to meet with your assessors in advance of the visit, and use the criteria in the EQA report form as a trial activity to see if you meet them. You should ensure you have evidence of achieving any action points. You will need to make sure that if you are asked something by an EQA and you answer yes, that you have the documentation and/or evidence to prove it.

Other aspects you could prepare in advance include informing reception staff to expect the EQA, informing the EQA about parking arrangements if they are travelling by car, and arranging a suitable room for the duration of the visit. All the required documents should be placed in the room (or be accessible), and all relevant staff should be available as needed.

At the end of the visit, the EQA should talk you through their findings and the content of their report. They should discuss any action and improvement points with you. Action points will be sanctionable if not met, whereas improvement points are just for development. The EQA might leave you with a copy of their report, or this might be sent to you via the AO afterwards, or be accessible online. Make sure you discuss the report with your team afterwards, and that you complete any action points by the agreed dates.

## Resources

- Previous EQA report
- Evidence of meeting any action points from the previous report
- All documents, learner evidence and records requested by the EQA

## Advantages

👍 Ensures you and your team are well prepared

👍 Can save time on the day of the visit by having a planned structure and everything readily available

## Disadvantages

👎 Relies on other staff providing the requested information and documentation to you well before the visit

👎 Some requested staff and learners might not be available for the visit at the last minute, thereby disrupting arrangements and highlighting a possible problem to the EQA

---

### Tip

Don't be afraid to challenge your EQA if they want to give you an action point which you don't agree with. They must be able to show you in writing, that what they are asking you to do, is officially part of the EQA process.

---

## Further reading and weblinks

Gravells A (2016) *Principles and Practices of Quality Assurance*. London: Learning Matters.

Pontin K (2012) *Practical Guide to Quality Assurance*. London: City & Guilds.

Read H (2011) *The Best Internal Quality Assurer's Guide*. Bideford: Read On Publications.

# 34  Producing resources

| IQA activity | √ | EQA activity | | Deep dive activity | * |
|---|---|---|---|---|---|
| In person | √ | Remote | * | Electronic/online | √ |
| Includes learners | √ | Includes assessors | √ | Includes others | * |
| Promotes standardisation | √ | Lead IQA role | √ | Quality improvement role | √ |

*depends upon what and how you are planning to use the approach*

## What is it?

Producing resources is about creating the required tools or aids which can support the learning, assessment, quality improvement and quality assurance processes. Resources can include books, documents, templates, handouts, videos, games, items of equipment, devices, objects, people, or any other relevant materials.

There might be a budget available to help purchase new resources, or you may have to produce your own or adapt someone else's, for example; their digital or paper-based resources. Producing resources as a team can help to standardise practice and therefore give a quality service to staff and learners.

Examples could include:

- assessment records such as action plans, tracking, and feedback documents
- internal quality assurance records such as planning, tracking, observation checklists, and feedback reports
- multi-choice questions, essay questions and quizzes with expected answers.
- standardised essay, dissertation, assignment or project assessment briefs.

Before any resources are used, they should go through a quality assurance process to ensure that they are:

- accessible or adaptive
- aimed at the correct level of learning and assessment
- checked for spelling, punctuation and grammar errors
- current
- fit for purpose
- meaningful
- original (i.e. not someone else's work as this is plagiarism if not correctly acknowledged)
- relevant.

If you are taking photocopies of a document, or parts of a journal or a book, you will need to make sure you are not breaching any copyright restrictions. Most qualification specifications from awarding organisations are usually copyright free.

Resources should be regularly evaluated for the impact they are having, and to ensure they are still fit for purpose. This could be carried out as part of a team meeting.

# What can it be used for?

Resources can be designed to support teachers with specific aspects of their role, for example: through a visual presentation, vlog or blog. They can provide a richer learning experience for learners by using alternative media which suits their needs, for example; an interactive digital activity rather than a paper-based one.

Alternatively, resources can be used for assessment and quality assurance purposes, such as templates and checklists which can help to standardise practice and focus decision making.

When creating templates, checklists and other documents, always include the date it was created and a version number, for example in a footer. Alternatively, or as well as, you could create a tracking document. This could include the document title, the date it was created, who created it, and when it will be reviewed and by whom.

Some staff training might be required to ensure that all staff are familiar with how to use the resources.

# Resources

- Some form of storage and tracking system to ensure only the latest versions of documents are accessible (manual and/or electronic)
- People; for example, freelance teachers and assessors if extra staff are required for particular subjects
- A budget for purchasing and adapting/updating resources

# Advantages

- Learning and assessment resources can be produced which are authentic and relevant
- Can support a particular quality assurance activity
- Can be designed to meet the needs of individual learners or staff

# Disadvantages

- Can take time to produce and check
- Depending on how they are created, they might not always look professional, or be of good quality

---

### Tip

Always take the time to check if any part of a written resource you are reviewing has been plagiarised or is subject to copyright restrictions.

---

# Further reading and weblinks

Atherton P (2018) *50 Ways to use Technology Enhanced Learning in the Classroom.* London: SAGE Publications.

Copyright – https://www.gov.uk/copyright

Gravells A (2017) *Principles and Practices of Teaching and Training.* London: Learning Matters.

Mansell S (2019) *50 Teaching and Learning Approaches.* London: Learning Matters.

Mansell S (2020) *50 Assessment Approaches.* London: Learning Matters.

Plagiarism – *About plagiarism* – www.plagiarism.org

# 35 Providing feedback

| IQA activity | √ | EQA activity | √ | Deep dive activity | * |
|---|---|---|---|---|---|
| In person | √ | Remote | √ | Electronic/online | √ |
| Includes learners | * | Includes assessors | √ | Includes others | * |
| Promotes standardisation | | Lead IQA role | √ | Quality improvement role | √ |

*depends upon what and how you are planning to use the approach

## What is it?

Providing feedback to someone can help with their motivation and development in their job role. It's about being constructive and developmental with your comments and advice, as and when necessary. Feedback can be given remotely via the telephone, email, online, or in person. However, it's best given face to face where possible so that a two-way conversation can take place and body language can be seen.

Informal feedback can be given at any time, perhaps when an assessor needs help with the way they agree assessment plans with their learners. Formal feedback should be given at an appropriate date, time and place, and in a constructive and developmental manner. It should never be critical of the person, but be based on the activities which have taken place. You should always give the person a copy of any report you have completed, for example; an internal quality assurance report for a sample you have carried out. This acts as a formal record and any agreed action points should always be followed up.

## What can it be used for?

Feedback can be used to support the development of staff, for example; as part of a quality improvement activity after an observation, or by an external quality assurer to an IQA to provide guidance as to how they can improve something.

If you find something that the person has done wrong, or could improve upon, don't be critical but state the facts. You could ask them to reflect upon their performance before you provide the feedback. This way, they might realise any mistakes before you have to point them out. You can then suggest ways of working together to put things right. It could be that they were unaware of something they should or should not have done. Communicating regularly and identifying any training needs could prevent problems from occurring. If you have a staff member who is performing really well, you could ask them to mentor an underperforming or new member of staff, providing they have the time.

Always allow time for the person to clarify anything you have said and for them to ask any questions. Don't interrupt them when they are speaking, and avoid jumping to any conclusions. Use eye contact and listen carefully to what they are saying. Show that you are a good listener by nodding your head and repeating key points. The person should leave knowing exactly what needs to be done and by when.

Feedback should always be (in alphabetical order):

- based on facts, not opinions
- clear, genuine and unambiguous
- constructive rather than destructive
- descriptive rather than evaluative
- developmental, giving examples for improvement or what could be changed
- documented, and with records maintained
- focused on the activity not the person
- helpful and supportive, guiding the person to useful resources and training activities
- honest and detailed regarding what was or wasn't carried out
- objective rather than subjective
- positive, focusing on what was good and how practice can be improved or changed
- specific and detailed
- strategic, and seeking to improve performance.

When providing feedback, if it's not all good, you will need to be aware that it could affect self-esteem. The quality of feedback received can be a key factor towards a person's motivation and development. Ongoing constructive feedback which is developmental and has been carefully thought through is an indication of your interest in the person, and of your intention to help them develop and do well in the future.

## Resources

- Written feedback records if given formally
- Action plan templates if relevant

## Advantages

👍 Allows a person to know how they are performing, what they are doing well, and what they need to improve or develop further

## Disadvantages

👎 If feedback is not given skillfully, it can have a negative effect on the person receiving it

**Tip**

Owning your statements by beginning with the word "*I*" should help the person focus on what you are saying. For example; "*I was able to see that you carried out that assessment very thoroughly by asking your learner several relevant questions.*" If you don't have any advice or action points to give, then don't create them just for the sake of it.

If you have to follow on with any negative points or criticisms, don't say "*But my only negative point is ...*" or "*But my only criticisms are ...*" It's much better to rephrase these words and say "*However, some areas for development could be ...*".

# Further reading and weblinks

Giving and receiving feedback – https://tinyurl.com/ya9ys8e9

Gravells A (2016) *Principles and Practices of Quality Assurance.* London: Learning Matters.

Pontin K (2012) *Practical Guide to Quality Assurance.* London: City & Guilds.

Read H (2012) *The Best Quality Assurer's Guide.* Bideford: Read On Publications.

# 36 Questioning others

| IQA activities | √ | EQA activities | √ | Deep dive activity | √ |
|---|---|---|---|---|---|
| In person | √ | Remote | √ | Electronic/online | √ |
| Includes learners | √ | Includes assessors | √ | Includes others | √ |
| Promotes standardisation | √ | Lead IQA role | √ | Quality improvement role | √ |

## What is it?

Questioning others is an activity which can help you gather extra quality evidence or information, check a person's knowledge and understanding, or to clarify something. It can be undertaken face to face or remotely.

Examples of different types of formal and informal questioning methods are:

1. Closed questioning (*Would you ...?*) – questions are posed which can be answered by a *yes* or *no* response. These types of responses don't demonstrate understanding.

2. Open questioning (*How would you ...?*) – questions are posed that cannot be answered by a simple *yes* or *no*.

3. Probing questions (*Why exactly was that?*) – often used after asking an open question to encourage someone to explore their initial answer and give more detail or information.

4. Recall and process questioning (*How did you ...?*) – questions are set around a particular job or task which requires the person to recall and process specific information before answering.

## What can it be used for?

Questioning can be used for both quality improvement and quality assurance activities with learners, staff, employers, witnesses and any others who are involved in the teaching, learning and/or assessment process. You can ask questions to individuals or to small groups, but you must ensure people feel sufficiently comfortable to answer the questions honestly. For example, a learner may not answer a question honestly if their teacher is present.

An example of using questioning with learners:

- If you were concerned about your safety what would you do?
- How do you keep yourself safe online? What training have you had?
- Tell me about the curriculum you follow?

- What are your teachers doing well?
- What can you do now that you couldn't do four months ago?
- What new skills and knowledge have you gained since starting the programme?

An example of using questioning with teaching and assessment staff:

- How are your learners progressing through the curriculum?
- How do you determine what a learner knows already and how do you fill the gaps in their knowledge?
- How have you been supported to develop your pedagogical knowledge?
- Tell me about the curriculum which your apprentices follow.
- What influence does the learner have regarding when they are assessed?
- What can your learners do now that they couldn't do four months ago?

An example of using questioning with an apprentice's employer:

- Does the standard of planned activities meet your requirements?
- How are you being supported to prepare your apprentice for their end-point assessment?
- What can your apprentice do now that they couldn't do four months ago?
- What influence did you have over the curriculum and subject/units selected?
- What involvement do you have in your apprentice's review process?

An example of questioning a witness from a learner's workplace:

- How do you keep your knowledge and skills up to date in relation to the qualification the learner is working towards?
- What qualifications and experience do you have in …?
- What training have you had to help you understand the qualification criteria and to write a witness testimony?
- What support or training would help you when writing a witness testimony?

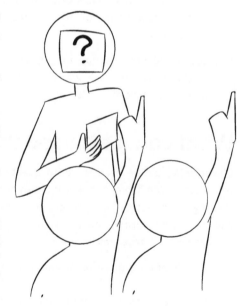

Questioning can also be used when undertaking joint work scrutiny (see Chapter 43) by asking the learners about a particular section of their work, e.g. how did your assessor's feedback help you to improve?

Data can also be used to validate the responses from the questions asked, e.g. attendance and achievement rates.

# Resources

- A bank of relevant open questions for each occasion

# Advantages

👍 Can be used in a wide variety of ways to suit individual needs

👍 Can support you to identify themes which may need probing further

# Disadvantages

👎 Questions must be open, otherwise you will only gain a *yes* or *no* response

👎 Questions must be unambiguous and relevant

> ## Tip
>
> To gain further information and evidence, you could use the triangulation approach by using different methods such as oral questions, questionnaires, and focus groups. This helps to validate the qualitative and quantitative data you receive.

# Further reading and weblinks

Geoff Petty – *Improve your teaching and that of your team* – https://tinyurl.com/lqusrxe

Gravells A (2017) *Principles and Practices of Teaching and Training.* London: Learning Matters.

Mansell S (2020) *50 Assessment Approaches.* London: Learning Matters.

Mind Tools – *Questioning techniques* – https://tinyurl.com/pehwshx

# 37 Reviewing and updating assessment activities

| IQA | √ | EQA | * | Deep dive activity | |
|---|---|---|---|---|---|
| In person | √ | Remote | √ | Electronic/online | * |
| Includes learners | * | Includes assessors | √ | Includes others | * |
| Promotes standardisation | √ | Lead IQA role | √ | Quality improvement role | * |

*depends upon what and how you are planning to use the approach

## What is it?

Reviewing and updating assessment activities is the responsibility of the lead internal quality assurer (IQA) and should be carried out on a regular basis, perhaps yearly. The review should include checking that the formative and summative assessment activities which are used, enable learners to meet the qualification or programme criteria. It also helps to standardise assessor practice by ensuring assessors interpret the requirements correctly and assess in a consistent way.

The assessment activities you should review and update could include those which are used for:

- assignment briefs
- initial, formative, summative and holistic assessment
- learner statements
- observations
- professional discussions
- portfolios of evidence
- question banks
- witness testimonies
- written tests or exams
- worksheets or workbooks.

## What can it be used for?

It can be used to ensure all assessment activities are fit for purpose.

During the review, which could be carried out during an IQA/assessor team meeting, you could use a checklist of relevant points for each of the assessment activities.

For example, a checklist for reviewing *question banks* might look like this:

- ☐ all questions are clearly stated and are not misleading in any way

- ☐ all questions cannot be misinterpreted in any way

- ☐ if there are multiple questions in a sentence, the questions should be separated into bullet points to ensure none can be missed

- ☐ expected responses for each question must have been agreed by all assessors

- ☐ all assessors understand both the questions and the expected responses, and what the minimum requirement for a correct response from a learner is

- ☐ all questions meet the requirements and content of the qualification or programme being assessed (the awarding organisation might need to be informed of any changes)

- ☐ the questions are robust, safe, valid, fair and reliable

- ☐ all questions are at the right level for what is being assessed

- ☐ if questions are to be graded, all staff agree on the grading criteria

- ☐ assessors are in agreement as to how many questions should be used for a test, e.g. 10

- ☐ there should be many more questions in the bank to allow for a random selection by assessors, therefore ensuring no two tests are the same

- ☐ all questions and expected responses must be stored safely and securely, to allow access only by authorised staff

If the team are in agreement of what works and what needs improving, a record should be kept of the discussion and an action plan created. This might be part of your role, or you could delegate some aspects to others. Don't forget to check that all action points have been met by the agreed dates.

You should include other relevant people when reviewing assessment activities, before updating or making any changes. These might include:

- • assessors
- • employers
- • learners
- • other IQAs
- • teachers or trainers
- • the EQA (if applicable)
- • witnesses.

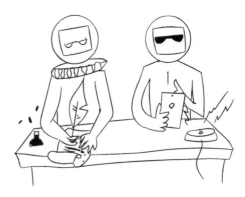

All staff will need to know about the changes, and training might be required if there are significant differences.

# Resources

- Relevant checklists
- Activities which are used for the assessment process
- A way of documenting what has been discussed and agreed, along with a subsequent action plan

# Advantages

👍 Ensures all assessment activities are current and fit for purpose

👍 Helps support standardisation by ensuring all staff are using the assessment activities consistently

# Disadvantages

👎 If the review is carried out by one person, it could be subjective

👎 Staff training might need to take place which could be time-consuming

👎 Some staff might not be aware of a change and continue to use outdated assessment activities

---

### Tip

If you are reviewing and updating assessment activities related to a vocational qualification or programme, you could check that these align to current industry practice by involving employers in the review process. For example, if you have learners who are undertaking work experience in a particular subject area, their employers might like to be involved.

---

# Further reading and weblinks

Gravells A (2016) *Principles and Practices of Quality Assurance*. London: Learning Matters.

Mansell S (2020) *50 Assessment Approaches*. London: Learning Matters.

# 38 Reviewing and updating internal quality assurance activities

| IQA activity | √ | EQA activity | | Deep dive activity | |
|---|---|---|---|---|---|
| In person | √ | Remote | √ | Electronic/online | √ |
| Includes learners | | Includes assessors | √ | Includes others | * |
| Promotes standardisation | √ | Lead IQA role | √ | Quality improvement role | * |

*depends upon what and how you are planning to use the approach

## What is it?

Reviewing and updating internal quality assurance (IQA) activities should be included as part of your organisation's quality policy. The activities should be reviewed regularly to check if they need updating, perhaps yearly.

The IQA activities which should be reviewed might include those for:

- sampling assessed learners' work and accompanying assessment records
- observing trainer and assessor practice
- talking to learners and/or others, e.g. witnesses from the workplace
- arranging team meetings
- arranging standardisation activities
- preparing for an external quality assurance visit.

## What can it be used for?

It can be used to ensure all IQA activities are current and fit for purpose.

During the review, which could be carried out during an IQA team meeting, you could use a checklist of relevant points for each of the IQA activities.

For example, a checklist for reviewing the activity of *sampling assessed learners' work and accompanying assessment records* might look like this:

Does the process ensure that (in alphabetical order):

☐ all assessment records are fully completed, i.e. plans and feedback records, and are dated and signed?

☐ all assessment types and methods are sampled?

☐ all assessors are using the correct documentation, records and templates?

☐ all the requirements have been met by the learner and the assessor has confirmed this to them?

☐ any trends found, e.g. learners making the same mistakes or assessors misinterpreting something, can be followed up?

☐ assessment feedback to learners is constructive and developmental, indicating what has been met and what still needs to be done?

☐ assessment planning is thorough and effective?

☐ assessors are consistent in their interpretation of what is being assessed?

☐ assessors are fully completing their records in a standardised way, including tracking sheets?

☐ assessors can receive support or further training if a need is identified

☐ feedback from others, e.g. employers and witnesses, is taken into consideration by assessors?

☐ good practice found from the sample can be shared between all assessors?

☐ if learners need any support or have any particular requirements, that these can be met?

☐ the assessment methods used are robust, safe, valid, fair and reliable?

☐ the learner evidence is valid, authentic, reliable, current and sufficient?

☐ the learner has been registered with the awarding organisation within the required timeframe (as any assessments prior to the registration date might be classed as invalid by an awarding organisation)?

☐ the learner's identity has been checked?

☐ there is a way to ensure assessors have implemented any action points from previous IQA reports?

☐ there is consistency of decisions between assessors for the same aspect sampled?

If the team are in agreement of what works and what needs improving, a record should be kept of the discussion and an action plan created. This might be part of your role, or you could delegate some aspects to others. Don't forget to check that all action points have been met by the agreed dates.

All staff will need to know about the changes, and training might be required if there are significant differences. Awarding organisations should also be notified of any changes to your IQA policies, systems and processes.

# Resources

- Relevant checklists
- Current documents or templates which are used for assessment and internal quality assurance
- A way of documenting what has been discussed and agreed, along with a subsequent action plan

# Advantages

⬆ Ensures all IQA activities are current and fit for purpose

⬆ Maintains compliance with relevant requirements

⬆ Helps support standardisation by ensuring all IQA staff are using the activities consistently

# Disadvantages

⬇ If the activity is carried out by one person, the review could be very subjective

⬇ Unless the review is added to a calendar of activities, it could be forgotten

⬇ Staff training might need to take place which could be time-consuming

⬇ Some staff might not be aware of a change and continue to use outdated documents

---

### Tip

If you are a lead IQA, you can add the activities and review dates to your work plan (see Chapter 49) to ensure there is a formal schedule.

---

# Further reading and weblinks

Gravells A (2016) *Principles and Practices of Quality Assurance*. London: Learning Matters.

Read H (2012) *The Best Quality Assurer's Guide*. Bideford: Read On Publications.

# 39 Sampling learners' work

| IQA activity | √ | EQA activity | √ | Deep dive activity | * |
|---|---|---|---|---|---|
| In person | √ | Remote | √ | Electronic/online | √ |
| Includes learners | | Includes assessors | | Includes others | |
| Promotes standardisation | √ | Lead IQA role | √ | Quality improvement | * |

*depends upon what and how you are planning to use the approach

## What is it?

Sampling learners' work is part of the internal and external quality assurance process. It can be done manually by physically looking at a learner's evidence along with the supporting assessment records; or it can be online if the work has been completed and uploaded electronically to a secure platform.

When sampling learners' work, you are not re-assessing or re-marking it. You are checking if the assessor has adequately planned and documented the assessment activities, made a correct decision, and provided constructive and developmental feedback to their learners. You need to make sure that all work is valid, authentic, reliable, current and sufficient (VARCS). If you are in any doubt, you must refer it back to the assessor. You should also authenticate learner and assessor signatures to ensure they are who they say they are. Your awarding organisation should give you advice regarding this.

Because you are only sampling, there will be some areas that get missed. This is a risk as you can't sample everything from everyone. You need to build up your confidence in the assessors to know that they are performing satisfactorily.

## What can it be used for?

It can be used to ensure that each assessor has correctly and fairly assessed their learners' work. When sampling work from different assessors, if you are sampling the same aspects, you can see how consistent they are. You can then note any inconsistencies and feed these back. For example, if one assessor is giving more support to learners, or expecting them to produce far more work than others, then this is clearly unfair. Some assessors might produce detailed assessment plans and another's might be minimal; the same might apply with the amount of feedback given.

You should always read the accompanying assessment plans and feedback records, and any other assessment records such as observation reports and witness testimonies. Reviewing all the assessment documentation will help you gain a clear picture of learner progress and achievement. If witnesses are used, you should contact a sample of these to confirm their authenticity, and that they understand what their role entails. If learner achievement relies heavily on the use of witness testimonies as evidence, then you, or someone else, might need to carry out adequate training and provide support to them.

You may agree with your assessor, in which case you can provide feedback as to what they have done well; you may agree, but feel your assessor could have given more developmental feedback to their learner. You can then give your assessor appropriate feedback as to how they could develop and improve. Alternatively, you might disagree with an assessor's decision and refer the work back to them. If this is the case, you would need to be very explicit as to why the work had not met the requirements, and give your assessor some advice regarding how they can support their learner towards achievement.

Other aspects to check for include the use of holistic planning and assessment. There's no need for an assessor to observe all the different units of a qualification separately, if one or two well-planned holistic observations will do. Another area to check is the recognition of prior learning (RPL). If a learner already holds an approved or accepted unit from another qualification, they should not have to repeat it.

If you find a problem when sampling, or have any concerns, you will need to increase your sample size. You can always carry out an additional random sample and ask to see something which isn't on your original plan. However, your decision can only be based upon what you have sampled and seen; you need to remain objective at all times.

Sampling learners' work is also a good opportunity to check for other things, for example, if plagiarism or copying is taking place. You should also check whether the learners have had the opportunity to be assessed in another language which is acceptable, for example, bilingually (e.g. English and/or Welsh or Gaelic). Some awarding organisations allow the use of an interpreter, but others don't; you would therefore need to find out what is acceptable.

Make sure you update your records (see Chapter 21) as you progress. A clear audit trail of all activities and actions must be maintained to assist compliance and transparency. It also helps in the event of an appeal or complaint.

## Resources

- Learner evidence and supporting assessment records
- Documentation such as a sampling plan, tracking sheet and quality assurance reports

# Advantages

👍 Ensures fairness and accuracy of assessment decisions

👍 Maintains compliance with the awarding organisation's requirements

👍 Contributes to the standardisation of assessor practice

# Disadvantages

👎 Can be time-consuming to plan for and carry out

---

### Tip

After a period of sampling, you could analyse your findings and provide overall feedback to your assessors, perhaps at the next team meeting. You might have found patterns or trends, for example, if all assessors are making the same mistake within a particular unit. An activity based on this can help towards the standardisation of assessment practice.

---

# Further reading and weblinks

Gravells A (2016) *Principles and Practices of Quality Assurance*. London: Learning Matters.

Plagiarism – www.plagiarism.org

Pontin K (2012) *Practical Guide to Quality Assurance*. London: City & Guilds.

Read H (2012) *The Best Quality Assurer's Guide*. Bideford: Read On Publications.

Wilson L (2012) *Practical Teaching: A Guide to Assessment and Quality Assurance*. Andover: Cengage Learning.

# 40 Shadowing staff

| IQA activity | √ | EQA activity | √ | Deep dive activity | √ |
|---|---|---|---|---|---|
| In person | √ | Remote | | Electronic/online | |
| Includes learners | * | Includes assessors | * | Includes others | * |
| Promotes standardisation | √ | Lead IQA role | | Quality improvement role | √ |

*depends upon what and how you are planning to use the approach*

## What is it?

Shadowing staff is an informal activity which is used to support or train someone for a particular job role or function. It is where a new or inexperienced member of staff (the shadowee) observes an experienced member of staff (the host) to learn from them, and develop their knowledge and skills.

Objectives or targets should be agreed between the host and the shadowee prior to the shadowing taking place. This helps to ensure everyone is using their time effectively and that the shadowee is developing the required knowledge and skills.

Shadowing could be carried out between two to five days where the shadowee observes the host carrying out their day-to-day job role or specific functions. This is followed up by a daily discussion to identify any areas which may need clarity. The shadowee should be encouraged to reflect on their experience and consider what else they feel they need to develop.

## What can it be used for?

Shadowing staff can be used to develop an individual's knowledge and skills for multiple purposes. For example, a new observer could shadow an experienced observer, or the lead internal quality assurer (IQA) could arrange for a new or inexperienced assessor to shadow an experienced assessor.

It is a great activity to include as part of the coaching and mentoring process (see Chapter 4) as it enables the shawdowee to observe first-hand how their mentor uses their knowledge and understanding to carry out specific roles, functions or responsibilities.

Shadowing staff can also be used for quality improvement purposes. For example, a person

undertaking the quality improvement role could informally shadow a member of staff to see how they perform a particular job role. This would help to provide ongoing support and development, as opposed to the process of a formal observation.

## Resources

- An experienced member of staff (the host)
- An inexperienced or new member of staff (the shadowee)

## Advantages

👍 Can help staff to reflect and learn from another's experience

👍 Can informally see how other staff or teams work

👍 Is an opportunity for personal development

👍 Can help to develop the host's coaching and mentoring skills

## Disadvantages

👎 Relies on the host being open to the activity

👎 Possibility of the shadowee picking up bad practice

---

### Tip

The shadowee could start to perform some of the roles they have been observing, whilst under the supervision of their host.

---

## Further reading and weblinks

University of Cambridge – *Personal and professional development job shadowing* – https://tinyurl.com/yd34e6g8

Thebalancecareers – *Job shadowing is effective on-the-job training* – https://tinyurl.com/yd45fzbu

# 41 Standardising practice

| IQA activity | √ | EQA activity | √ | Deep dive activity | |
|---|---|---|---|---|---|
| In person | √ | Remote | √ | Electronic/online | √ |
| Includes learners | | Includes assessors | √ | Includes others | √ |
| Promotes standardisation | √ | Lead IQA role | √ | Quality improvement role | √ |

## What is it?

Standardising practice is all about ensuring reliability and fairness of practice between all staff who are involved in a particular subject area. This should enable a consistent experience for all learners from the time they commence to the time they achieve or leave. Standardisation enables people to work as a team rather than on their own, and to give an equitable service to all learners. It is also an opportunity to ensure all staff are interpreting the qualification and programme requirements accurately.

It's also a good way of maintaining professional development and ensuring compliance and accountability with awarding organisations' and regulatory authorities' requirements.

It's important to standardise practice to be fair to all learners. For example, if you assess a vocational qualification you might decide to carry out two observations with each of your learners and give them a written test. Whereas another assessor might only carry out one observation and ask a few oral questions. There are times when an individual learner's needs should be taken into account which will lead to a difference in assessment activities. However, all learners should be entitled to the same assessment experience, regardless of which assessor they have been allocated.

## What can it be used for?

Attending a standardisation event will give you the opportunity to share good practice and compare your decisions with those of your colleagues. This will ensure you have interpreted the requirements accurately, that the learner evidence is appropriate, and that the supporting records are completed correctly. Even if you don't learn anything new, it will hopefully confirm you are doing things correctly. It's also a requirements if you offer an accredited qualification. Please see Appendix 2 for an example completed standardisation record for assessed work.

Standardisation events are not team meetings; the latter are to discuss issues relating to the management of the programme such as targets, achievement rates and learner issues.

The events can be led by assessors, internal and external quality assurers, e.g. to standardise the way reports are completed.

Standardisation activities can include:

- agreeing the interpretation of qualification requirements (or what is to be taught/assessed)
- collaborating on schemes of work, session plans, course materials and resources
- comparing how documents and records have been completed
- creating assessment activities, materials, assignments, questions and recommended answers
- designing or revising assessment and quality assurance documents
- discussing decisions made by other assessors/IQAs
- discussing the qualification/programme/job requirements
- interpreting policies and procedures
- new staff shadowing experienced staff
- peer observations and feedback to ensure consistency of practice
- preparing materials for induction and initial assessments
- role-play activities such as assessment planning, making a decision, giving feedback, dealing with a complaint (and visually recording for later viewing).

Technology can be used for standardisation purposes and is ideal if not all the team members can attend a meeting or an activity at the same time, or are located in different buildings. When standardising the decisions assessors have made based on electronic evidence, it's important to be sure the work does belong to the learner, and that the assessor has confirmed its authenticity.

Some examples of using technology for standardisation purposes include:

- holding meetings via Skype or video-conferencing facilities to discuss the interpretation of aspects of a programme or qualification
- using online webinars to help standardise delivery and assessment approaches
- creating, updating and sharing documents online, e.g. schemes of work, session plans and course materials
- making visual recordings of how to complete forms and reports: if a staff member is unsure how to fill in a form they could access a video to see an example
- visually recording standardisation activities and uploading them to an intranet or virtual learning environment (VLE) for viewing/listening to later.

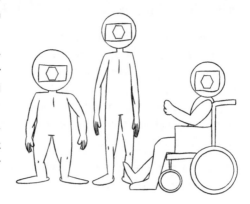

# Resources

- Standardisation template
- Qualification specification and/or programme handbook
- Copies of completed documents to be used as a basis for discussion

# Advantages

👍 Ensures all staff are interpreting and documenting the requirements correctly

👍 Gives a fair service to all learners

# Disadvantages

👎 Can be difficult to get all relevant staff together at the same time

👎 If some staff are not aware of what has been standardised, they might make mistakes

---

### Tip

Keep up to date with any changes regarding qualification or programme content, as it is usually revised every few years. Awarding organisations will issue regular updates and these can be used as a standardisation activity.

---

# Further reading and weblinks

Gravells A (2016) *Principles and Practices of Quality Assurance*. London: Learning Matters.

Pontin K (2012) *Practical Guide to Quality Assurance*. London: City & Guilds.

Read H (2012) *The Best Quality Assurer's Guide*. Bideford: Read On Publications.

Ann Gravells – *Standardisation* – https://tinyurl.com/y8xg66h8

Wilson L (2012) *Practical Teaching: A Guide to Assessment and Quality Assurance*. Andover: Cengage Learning.

# 42    Undertaking evaluation activities

| IQA activity | √ | EQA activity | √ | Deep dive activity | * |
|---|---|---|---|---|---|
| In person | √ | Remote | √ | Electronic/online | √ |
| Includes learners | √ | Includes assessors | √ | Includes others | * |
| Promotes standardisation | √ | Lead IQA role | * | Quality improvement role | * |

*depends upon what and how you are planning to use the approach

## What is it?

Evaluation is about measuring the effectiveness of something, e.g. the assessment and quality assurance activities. The evaluation process includes obtaining feedback from others, as well as gathering and analysing data. The overall result should be to help you improve your own practice, the practice of others, and the learner experience.

Evaluation is a quality improvement tool for a *product* or a *service*. If your organisation offers a qualification or a programme of learning, then that is the *product*. The facilities of the organisation and the support your learners receive relate to the *service*. Your learners should have the opportunity to evaluate the products and services at some point, perhaps by completing a questionnaire or survey (see Chapter 14).

Activities can include those to measure aspects relating to:

- self-evaluation
- peer evaluation
- learner evaluation
- employee evaluation
- programme evaluation.

Self-evaluation is about considering what you are doing well and what you can improve. It can involve completing a learning journal or a diary which demonstrates how you dealt with critical incidents and what you would do differently next time. It can also be a standardised approach within an organisation by the use of a pre-prepared template with specific questions. Self-evaluation can be in isolation from other areas of evaluation, or link to employee evaluation.

Peer evaluation is about observing others in their role, and then discussing what was good about it, and what could be done differently or improved. A pre-prepared template or observation checklist could be designed and used.

Learner evaluation is about obtaining feedback regarding the products and services offered. A questionnaire could be given to learners at the end of a session to gain specific comments as to how the session went. Alternatively, feedback can be obtained via a survey regarding a specific service, such as the learning resource facilities.

Employee evaluation is about giving your staff the opportunity to discuss their progress regarding their job role. It can include appraisals and performance reviews. It can be a valuable opportunity to discuss learning and development, training and support, and to set performance targets. It is also a chance to reflect upon achievements and successes.

Programme evaluation is about obtaining feedback from learners (and others involved) regarding the way a particular course has been managed and implemented. Surveys can take place at several points, e.g. after the induction process, part way through, and/or at the end.

# What can it be used for?

It can be used as an ongoing way of gaining feedback and making improvements throughout all aspects of teaching, learning, assessment and quality assurance. The process can be informal by talking to others or formal by using a questionnaire or survey. Either way, the process should help you realise how effective things are, and what you could change or improve. It will also help you identify any problem areas, enabling you to do things differently next time.

Using feedback from others and gaining information and data are key to a good evaluation process. Never assume everything is going well just because you think it is.

You can do this by:

- carrying out questionnaires and surveys with all involved
- analysing data and statistics such as enrolment, retention, achievement, destinations and progression
- analysing appeals and complaints
- talking to relevant people and agencies
- looking for trends or patterns to find out why things are occurring, e.g. several assessors are misinterpreting the number of observations required for a particular aspect of a qualification.

Once you have obtained and analysed the feedback, information and data, you should create an action plan with appropriate target dates, and notify all relevant staff of your findings and intentions.

# Resources

- Pre-prepared questionnaires and/or surveys
- Templates and checklists
- A means of analysing data such as computer software or apps

# Advantages

👍 Involves and includes all staff

👍 Enables people to have their voice heard

👍 Leads to an improvement in the products and services offered

# Disadvantages

👎 Not all staff may have the time to implement the activities fully

👎 Some people might not be totally honest with their responses, particularly for self-evaluation where they think they are doing better than they are

👎 If you choose to implement all the activities online, this would disadvantage anyone who does not have access or the confidence to use an online device

---

### Tip

When designing evaluation activities, involve others by asking them how they would approach the process. Be prepared to change your ideas and/or to consider other ways of doing something.

---

# Further reading and weblinks

Kirkpatrick D & Kirkpatrick J (2006) *Evaluating Training Programs*. Oakland: Berrett-Koehler Publishers.

Online surveys – *www.surveymonkey.com* and *www.smartsurvey.co.uk*

Questionnaire design – https://tinyurl.com/mfqvc23

Roffey-Barentsen J and Malthouse R (2013) *Reflective Practice in Education and Training* (2nd edn). London: Learning Matters.

Self-evaluation – https://tinyurl.com/yyepuyxu

Stufflebeam D & Coryn C (2007) *Evaluation Theory, Models and Applications*. San Francisco: Jossey-Bass.

Wood J and Dickinson J (2011) *Quality Assurance and Evaluation in the Lifelong Learning Sector*. Exeter: Learning Matters.

# 43 Undertaking joint work scrutiny

| Internal activity | * | External activity | √ | Deep dive activity | √ |
|---|---|---|---|---|---|
| In person | √ | Remote | √ | Electronic/online | √ |
| Includes learners | √ | Includes assessors | √ | Includes others | √ |
| Promotes standardisation | * | Lead IQA role | √ | Quality Improvement | √ |

*depends upon what and how you are planning to use the approach*

## What is it?

Joint work scrutiny is a collaborative approach between teachers, learners, quality improvement and quality assurance staff. The process can be used to check the quality of a learning programme, and to support consistency and standardisation of practice amongst staff. It includes activities that can be carried out with learners. These can contribute to quality assurance measures, and to identify actions and improvements.

The main focus of joint work scrutiny is carried out by a quality reviewer checking the learning and the progress that is or has taken place with individuals, or a small group of learners. The process could include:

- learners showing the quality reviewer their portfolio of evidence (paper based or online) and explaining what knowledge, skills, behaviours and attitudes, in relation to their learning programme, they have developed over time
- learners or teachers discussing with the quality reviewer the individual learning plans (ILP) and review documents they use, identifying what they know now that they didn't know before (paper based or online)
- learners showing the quality reviewer their course notes and explaining how their teachers support them in keeping their notes accurate.

Joint work scrutiny is not a stand-alone quality assurance check. It should be used to triangulate evidence of learning with other activities, such as the quality reviewer:

- observing teaching and learning approaches and activities
- visiting learning environments
- checking assessment records
- discussing the context of a scheme of work with the teacher and how the planned tasks and activities contribute to the learning process.

For example, after observing a teacher you could interview them and their learners to discuss the curriculum and how the learners are progressing. It is also an opportunity to discuss the sequencing of learning, i.e. why a topic is being delivered at a particular point, and how prior knowledge and skills are being incorporated into the sessions.

## What can it be used for?

Joint work scrutiny activities should be used to check the following:

- are learners' knowledge and skills being developed in a logical sequence to enable them to progress over time?

- does the content of the programme cover a suitable depth and breadth of topics within the subject?

- what progress have learners made from their starting point? (i.e. what do they know now that they didn't know before?)

- are learners given regular opportunities to revisit previous learning to enable them to recall information and commit knowledge, skills, behaviours and attitudes to their long-term memory?

- are any misconceptions appropriately addressed?

Joint work scrutiny can be used formally or informally; it can be a quality improvement or a quality assurance approach depending on the findings. If issues are discovered, training and support should be put in place to enable staff to improve and develop their practice.

## Resources

- Depends on how you are using the approach

## Advantages

👍 Enables a measure of learner progress over time

👍 Focuses on what the learners are actually learning and its relevance to the subject

👍 Supports standardisation

👍 Can be used as a reference point for training and development to improve practice

# Disadvantages

☞ Can make some learners anxious, or feel they have to be biased in favour of the member of staff

☞ Not all subjects are suitable for work scrutiny (e.g. modern languages might be spoken, not written)

☞ Not a suitable approach at the beginning of the programme

---

### Tip

When speaking to the learners, you should ask them; *what can you do now that you couldn't do before you started your programme of study?* This will help you to know how they are progressing.

---

# Further reading and weblinks

For Schools Education Services – *The New Ofsted Criteria and Work Scrutiny* – https://tinyurl.com/wlq4jea

Workbook scrutiny – https://tinyurl.com/yyjycref

Learning Cultures CPD for Teachers – *Preparing for subject specific deep dive conversations and observations* – https://tinyurl.com/w2k48k8

# 44 Undertaking peer observations

| IQA activity | √ | EQA activity | √ | Deep dive activity | |
|---|---|---|---|---|---|
| In person | √ | Remote | * | Electronic/online | * |
| Includes learners | √ | Includes assessors | √ | Includes others | √ |
| Promotes standardisation | * | Lead IQA role | * | Quality improvement role | * |

*depends upon what and how you are planning to use the approach

## What is it?

Peer observation is about one teacher observing another teacher delivering a session to their learners. It is a non-judgmental two-way process to develop and improve teaching practice. It can benefit both the peer observer and the teacher being observed, as they can learn from each other. After observing a session, the peer observer informally provides feedback to the peer observee, who in turn reflects on the feedback received. They can then make improvements to their future practice.

Although peer observations mainly relate to teachers, assessors, internal and external quality assurers could carry it out amongst themselves to aid the standardisation of practice.

As an organisational approach, teachers should be paired in accordance to their needs and/or subjects taught. There is no set time of how long the peer observation should take, it could be to observe the full session or just part of the session. The pair may also decide to observe each other more than once.

Peer observation can be subject related or non-subject related depending on the required outcome. For example, peer observation between subject specialists enables them to share specific details, whereas non-specialist teachers can share teaching practice pedagogical approaches.

## What can it be used for?

Peer observation is a great quality improvement tool. It enables teachers to informally share their teaching practice knowledge and skills, and then reflect together on how they can both further improve their performance.

Pairing of teachers can vary depending on the organisation's needs, for example:

- an experienced teacher could observe an inexperienced teacher to provide informal feedback and support

- an inexperienced teacher could observe an experienced teacher

- teachers could choose who they want to peer observe

- experienced teachers could observe each other to share pedagogy principles and practices

- subject specialists could observe each other to share knowledge and skills.

Peer observation can be used in any context, e.g. in a classroom, workshop or training room, and could be with a group of learners or an individual learner. However, if it's with an individual learner, it might be best to ask them first, as they may be nervous with another person there. The learners should be informed that the peer observer is not looking at what they are doing, but what the teacher is doing. The critical factor is that teachers are facilitating and improving the learning process.

## Resources

- Depends upon what and how you are planning to use the approach, e.g. a checklist could be used between the peers to aid standardisation of the observation process

## Advantages

👍 Most teachers see peer observation as non-threatening

👍 Encourages teachers to try out a range of different approaches by learning from each other

👍 Helps to prepare the observee for formal observations

👍 Can be documented as part of a teacher's continuing professional development (CPD)

## Disadvantages

👎 Peer feedback can be biased

👎 Not all teachers see it as important or useful activity

👎 Learners might act differently with another person in the room

---

Tip

You could design a template for teachers to use to document the observation. However, this may make them feel the process is too formal and they may not be as open to share their thoughts and ideas. The teachers might like to design their own checklist, which could be more appropriate to what they want to achieve from the peer observation process.

---

# Further reading and weblinks

British Council – *Peer observation* – https://tinyurl.com/y9v52xtr

Cambridge Assessment International Education – *Getting started with peer observation* – https://tinyurl.com/wgad36e

# 45 Updating staff

| IQA activity | √ | EQA activity | √ | Deep dive activity | |
|---|---|---|---|---|---|
| In person | √ | Remote | √ | Electronic/online | √ |
| Includes learners | | Includes assessors | √ | Includes others | √ |
| Promotes standardisation | √ | Lead IQA role | √ | Quality improvement role | √ |

## What is it?

Updating staff is a key element to managing an effective team, and will ensure they are all working to current internal and external requirements. The education, skills and training sector is fast moving with frequent and sometimes substantial updates and changes taking place. You might encounter a wide range of these, many of which are influenced by external and internal factors.

External factors which could influence internal processes include, but are not limited to:

- funding updates (publicly funded organisations only)
- awarding organisation (AO) updates to qualifications, assessment, policies or procedures
- government initiatives or decrees
- regulatory updates and inspection changes, e.g. Ofqual and/or Ofsted.

Examples of internal updates you may need to share with staff could include:

- informing relevant staff regarding revised or new policies and/or procedures and practices
- notifying everyone in the organisation regarding the revised opening hours for access to rooms and buildings
- informing your team of staff leaving and/or new staff joining
- notifying variations to individuals' roles and responsibilities
- updating staff regarding a new curriculum offer or the removal of a curriculum offer
- telling staff about increased or decreased curriculum or programme hours
- introducing staff to a different awarding organisation's or stakeholder's requirements
- notifying staff regarding budget, finance and resource changes
- updating staff regarding safeguarding arrangements.

An ideal way to keep yourself and your team updated regarding external organisations' changes, is to sign up to any updating services which may be offered. For example, most awarding organisations (AO) offer a mailing list service which staff can sign up to, to receive relevant updates from them by email.

The Department for Education also offer a mailing list service. They are responsible for children's services and education and are supported by several other agencies and public bodies including Ofqual and Ofsted. When you register for the updates, only select the areas you need to, as there could be around 40 to 60 changes per week if you sign up for them all.

# What can it be used for?

To manage an effective team, it is of vital importance that staff are kept up to date with relevant information which affects their role and responsibilities.

Examples of this include:

A lead internal quality assurer (IQA) being responsible for disseminating and discussing changes or updates from awarding organisations. This information should go to IQAs, assessors and any others involved in the assessment process. This could include updates to policies, procedures and/or qualification content.

If your provision receives public funding, the qualifications you offer must be listed on the Learning Aim Reference Service (LARS) to receive it. The LARS database is updated regularly with qualifications being added and removed. Part of the lead IQA's role will be to check if any proposed new qualifications are on the list, or if any of the current qualifications offered are due to be removed from the list. The lead IQA should share this information with their manager to enable decisions to be made with regard to the curriculum offer.

A quality improvement role to monitor government initiatives or decrees and regulatory changes and updates. For example, updating internal safeguarding policies and procedures and training staff regarding the changes. This will be influenced by government guidance using updates from the document *Keeping Children Safe in Education* (at least annually for learners who are 18 years and under). Part of the quality improvement role is the responsibility for updating internal policies and procedures to reflect any changes, disseminate the information to the relevant staff, and offer support and training opportunities.

An IQA informing their team of assessors about a change to the assessment plan template they must use. The IQA would need to ensure that all assessors can no longer access the previous version.

There are many methods you can use to update your staff including:

- email or a printed memo
- team meetings (face to face or online)
- text message
- verbal (face to face, telephone or online)
- social media
- staff intranet
- noticeboards (physical or electronic).

You will need to choose the methods which are most suited to the situation and the staff members. See Chapter 5 for more ideas regarding how you can effectively communicate the updates to your staff.

# Resources

- Access to any internal or external updates
- Methods to communicate the updates to staff

# Advantages

👍 Supports compliance

👍 Improves quality, providing all staff follow the updates

👍 Ensures staff are standardising their practice

# Disadvantages

👎 Can be time-consuming to check that all relevant staff have understood and are implementing the changes and updates

---

**Tip**

As soon as you find out that something has changed, make sure you communicate it to all relevant staff. If you leave it a while, and it relates to something urgent or important, staff will not be aware of it and problems could occur.

---

# Further reading and weblinks

HM Government – *Learning Aim Reference Service (LARS)* – https://tinyurl.com/y8mqp9mg

The Key for School Leaders – *Changes and challenges in education*– https://tinyurl.com/y958reu3

Ofqual – https://tinyurl.com/o3bypv7

Ofsted – https://tinyurl.com/lczdnn8

# 46 Using a strengths, weaknesses, opportunities and threats (SWOT) analysis

| IQA activity | √ | EQA activity | | Deep dive activity | |
|---|---|---|---|---|---|
| In person | √ | Remote | √ | Electronic/online | √ |
| Includes learners | * | Includes assessors | √ | Includes others | * |
| Promotes standardisation | √ | Lead IQA role | √ | Quality improvement role | √ |

*depends upon what and how you are planning to use the approach

## What is it?

A SWOT analysis is a technique for assessing four aspects of your practice, and these are strengths, weaknesses, opportunities and threats, hence the acronym SWOT. It supports you to identify how you can improve your practice and reduce the chances of poor practice or failure, by understanding what you do well and what you need to change. It also helps to eliminate, where possible, any problems or issues which may catch you unaware, and identify openings to improve your practice.

Strengths and weaknesses could be considered as internal, i.e. within your organisation, whereas opportunities and threats could be considered as external. Strengths and opportunities can be helpful, whereas weaknesses and threats can be harmful.

For example:

- strengths (*What do you do well, what is unique about what you do?*): I am an experienced well-qualified individual and part of an outstanding performing team. I use high quality resources which encourage learning and promote assessment opportunities.

- weaknesses (*What needs to improve?*): I am not always on time at completing some identified action points.

- opportunities (*What opportunities are open to you?*): I could develop the curriculum and gain accreditation for a new qualification to support a local need.

- threats (*What threats could harm your practices?*): If, during an external quality assurance visit or an external inspection, they identify something I was not aware of.

A good way to start the SWOT analysis is to design a matrix with four boxes. Each box should be given one of the four titles – strengths, weaknesses, opportunities and threats – as below. Under each title, you can list your thoughts.

| **S**trengths | **W**eaknesses |
|---|---|
| **O**pportunities | **T**hreats |

Once you have completed the SWOT analysis, you will need to act on the results. This can be by applying the strengths and planning how you will implement the opportunities to improve your practice. In addition, you will need to plan how you will minimise or eliminate the risks from the weaknesses and threats.

# What can it be used for?

A SWOT analysis can be used for products, services, resources, projects and people. It can help to identify the advantages and disadvantages which contribute to certain factors, and can be individual or group led. It is used to help improve practice, and is useful for identifying strengths and weaknesses as well as opportunities and threats for any aspect of a job role and/or an organisation's business operation.

A SWOT analysis is a great tool for self-assessment, and/or to improve the performance of a team. It can be used to help define an overall organisation strategy or an element of strategy, such as marketing, or the recruitment of new staff or learners. It can also be used to develop the curriculum you offer, and support the evidencing of why you have chosen to do something.

# Resources

- A SWOT matrix
- A method of documenting your findings from the SWOT analysis

# Advantages

👍 Can help to identify new solutions to problems

👍 Can help to discover possibilities and limitations for change

👍 Simple to use and cost effective

# Disadvantages

👎 Can be subjective

👎 Is only as good as the thoughts and ideas people put into it

---

### Tip

Depending on how you plan to use the SWOT analysis, you may find it useful to include as many members of your team as possible. This is to enable different views to be taken into consideration.

---

# Further reading and weblinks

British Library – *Bright ideas inspiring people* – https://tinyurl.com/yct9hqww

CIPD – SWOT Analysis Tips – https://tinyurl.com/ybz9so2y

Fine L (2009) *The SWOT Analysis: Using your Strength to Overcome Weaknesses, Using Opportunities to Overcome Threats.* CreateSpace, Independent Publishing Platform.

Gravells A (2016) *Principles and Practices of Quality Assurance.* London: Learning Matters.

# 47 Using role play

| IQA activity | √ | EQA activity | √ | Deep dive activity | |
|---|---|---|---|---|---|
| In person | √ | Remote | | Electronic/online | |
| Includes learners | * | Includes assessors | √ | Includes others | * |
| Promotes standardisation | √ | Lead IQA role | √ | Quality improvement role | √ |

*depends upon what and how you are planning to use the approach*

## What is it?

Role play is a technique which allows staff to explore different situations which they may encounter as part of their job role, in a safe and realistic but supportive situation. It enables them to develop skills and strategies which will help them in the future, by assuming the role of another person and acting out a scenario.

For example:

- an EQA could role play how to agree action points with an IQA in a centre
- an IQA could role play how they provide feedback to an assessor who has misinterpreted something
- an assessor could role play as though they are a learner who has not yet met the requirements of a unit; another assessor could provide feedback explaining why the learner hadn't met the requirements and what they need to do to improve
- a teacher could role play a difficult or challenging learner who is easily distracted, whilst another teacher tries different methods of engagement to persuade the learner to remain on task.

A role play activity should be followed by a discussion and feedback which identifies what went well and what could have gone better.

## What can it be used for?

Role play is a great way to develop your staff's confidence and skills in a safe environment. It is designed to enable the development of problem-solving skills, such as responding to difficult situations, and to develop best practice. It can be used for standardisation purposes, and is a brilliant activity to use with new or inexperienced teachers or assessors. Clear roles and time limits will need to be defined prior to starting the activity.

Observing an individual undertaking a role play activity will enable you to see them demonstrate their current skills, knowledge and understanding. You can see how they react in different situations and identify any further training or development which may be needed.

Pairs or small groups of staff could act out a scenario and be observed by their peers, who could then ask questions and/or provide feedback. This would help develop observation, questioning and communication skills. In addition, the role play scenarios could be visually recorded and used for future training and development, standardisation purposes, and for new staff to view. They could be uploaded to a secure area of the organisation's intranet to enable staff members to view them in their own time.

## Resources

- A suitable room to undertake the activity
- Role-play scenarios
- Recording equipment (if visually recording)

## Advantages

- Empowers staff to demonstrate their current skills and knowledge
- Enables staff to practise new skills in a safe, realistic and supportive setting
- Helps staff to see how things should/should not be done
- Allows decision making and problem solving to be observed and discussed
- Develops understanding from a different perspective

## Disadvantages

- Can be difficult to engage staff who are easily embarrassed
- Can quickly become disorganised if not kept under control
- Not all staff will take it seriously
- If being recorded, all staff will need to agree to it

> ### Tip
>
> A short reflective activity could be completed after the role play to enable staff to identify at least one thing they would do differently based on the experience.

# Further reading and weblinks

British Council – *Role-play* – https://tinyurl.com/yytor9k3

Mansell S (2019) *50 Teaching and Learning Approaches*. London: Learning Matters.

Mansell S (2020) *50 Assessment Approaches*. London: Learning Matters.

# 48 Using web conferences, online meetings and webinars

| IQA activity | √ | EQA activity | √ | Deep dive activity | |
|---|---|---|---|---|---|
| In person | | Remote | √ | Electronic/online | √ |
| Includes learners | √ | Includes assessors | √ | Includes others | √ |
| Promotes standardisation | * | Lead IQA role | * | Quality improvement role | * |

*depends upon what and how you are planning to use the approach

## What is it?

A web conference (sometimes called video conferencing or an online meeting) is a two-way communication method which allows the presenter to be seen and to speak to one or more remote participants in real time. It is live and relies on a strong and reliable internet connection. Each participant must have a suitable device and equipment, with access to relevant programs or apps. This should include a microphone, speakers and a video camera. Most modern laptops and smartphones include these features. The participants can choose whether to switch their cameras on and be seen by everyone, or to switch on audio only just to be heard. Alternatively, they can leave their camera and audio off and just listen and watch. Web conferences can be recorded and shared with a wider audience later on. However, because it is recorded live it is harder to make a high-quality video, and everyone would need to be in agreement to being recorded.

A webinar (sometimes called a web-based seminar or webcast) is usually a one-way communication method which allows the presenter to be seen and to speak to remote participants. A webinar allows very little interaction between the presenter and the participants and is often used as a training tool. A webinar can be delivered live and participants can key in questions into a textbox or a chat window. The presenter can select and read relevant questions out loud and then answer them. However, a webinar is often presented and pre-recorded to enable participants to access it at a time to suit them, which does not allow for any interaction.

Both methods of communication are types of *online collaborative services* which allow the presenter to share their computer screen to show a presentation, images, documents and/or text to the participants. Some web-conferencing applications allow the participants to share their computer screens with others. It's best to use passwords and security features when using web conferencing.

# What can it be used for?

It works well as a remote platform for meetings, and to keep staff up to date and informed regarding any changes from awarding organisations or regulators, or to update staff regarding changes to legislation, policies and procedures. It could also be used to provide generic feedback to teachers and assessors after an internal quality assurance activity.

For example:

- web conferencing is a great tool to deliver live training or carry out standardisation activities remotely
- online meetings are brilliant for teams who struggle to meet face to face due to distance, time or other constraints
- webinars are an exceptionally cost-effective way to deliver training to reach a large number of participants in a short timescale.

There are many different communication applications available to download, or platforms to use. Some are free to use and some require a subscription. However some are not classed as being secure and can easily be hacked. This risks breaching data protection, or inappropriate images or adverts hijacking a live streaming.

# Resources

- Technical equipment to enable participation by all parties
- Data storage and/or a way of recording and saving the webinar
- Editing equipment or apps (if applicable for the webinar)

# Advantages

👍 Cost effective
👍 Can reach a wide audience
👍 Is flexible as it is not reliant on participants travelling to a venue
👍 Can be fun and engaging
👍 Webinars can be recorded which enables wider access for later viewing

# Disadvantages

👎 Relies on everyone having access to relevant electronic devices and a strong and reliable internet connection

ᗑ Can be time-consuming to organise

ᗑ Technical support may be required

ᗑ Web conferences are difficult to manage if everyone is trying to talk at the same time

---

### Tip

Allow yourself at least ten to fifteen minutes before the commencement of a live communication, to log in and test that everything is working correctly, before your participants join you.

---

# Further reading and weblinks

PEDIAA – *What is the difference between webinar and video conference?* – https://tinyurl.com/yahnljjj

Zoom – *Meeting and webinar comparisons* – https://tinyurl.com/rb9nejn

# 49  Using work plans

| IQA activity | √ | EQA activity | √ | Deep dive activity | * |
|---|---|---|---|---|---|
| In person | √ | Remote | √ | Electronic/online | √ |
| Includes learners | | Includes assessors | √ | Includes others | √ |
| Promotes standardisation | | Lead IQA role | √ | Quality improvement role | √ |

## What is it?

A work plan is a visual reminder of what needs to be done and when, by yourself and the others in your team. When you are delegating tasks to team members, having a work plan will help ensure you allocate the work fairly and effectively. Monitoring and reviewing the activities as they are carried out will ensure appropriate progress is being made. The tasks should lead to an improvement in the quality and standards of the product or service being offered. The product could be a qualification or a programme of learning, the service could be the support which underpins teaching, learning and assessment. Records should always be maintained of all activities carried out for tracking and audit purposes, and for external inspections if required.

If you currently carry out internal or external quality assurance activities or have a quality improvement role, you might already be using some types of work plans such as:

- an observation plan
- a meeting and standardisation plan
- a sample plan and tracking sheet.

A work plan will help you to prioritise and keep track of all your objectives and the activities required to meet them. If you manage a team, you should discuss and agree these with your staff members rather than impose objectives and activities on them.

## What can it be used for?

It can be used to help you to plan how to meet the objectives which need to be carried out, the various activities required to meet them, and the dates by which they need to be completed.

An example objective could be: *plan, monitor and review the internal quality assurance (IQA) process in accordance with organisational requirements.*

Your work plan would then list certain activities such as:

- *create an IQA sampling plan*
- *plan dates for team meetings*
- *prepare for an external quality assurance visit.*

See Appendix 3 for a completed example of a work plan. A date is added to the shaded area once the activity has taken place.

Alternative styles of work plan could be used, e.g. wall planners, or templates such as Gantt charts which are available free via an internet search, or as part of some computer programs and apps. A Gannt chart is so called as it is named after Henry Gantt (1861–1919) and is a type of bar chart used to illustrate a project schedule.

Information you might need to help create a work plan includes (in alphabetical order):

- details of your team members, what their experience, knowledge and skills are, and what they are expected to do and when
- financial information such as budgets
- information regarding what is being assessed and quality assured
- a job description (or role specification) for yourself and others you are responsible for
- objectives to be met
- the organisation's vision and mission
- priorities, targets and expected success criteria
- relevant documentation, policies and procedures
- relevant requirements to offer qualifications (if applicable)
- resources, physical and human, and other aspects such as transport and availability of resources
- the locations and contact details of your team members and other relevant staff.

Using the *who, what, when, where, why* and *how* (WWWWWH) approach will help you to create your work plans. All tasks and activities you set for yourself and your team should have objectives which are SMART, i.e. specific, measurable, achievable, relevant, and time bound.

# Resources

- Work plan template or other document
- Information regarding staff roles and responsibilities
- List of objectives and activities to be carried out

# Advantages

👍 Ensures all objectives are planned for, carried out and monitored

👍 Utilises the strengths of team members for various activities

# Disadvantages

👎 If you don't agree the objectives and activities with your team, the staff will feel you have imposed them, and they might not be as motivated to achieve these

---

### Tip

You, and your team members, could carry out a SWOT analysis to ascertain strengths, weaknesses, opportunities and threats. This can help when discussing and allocating activities (see Chapter 46).

---

# Further reading and weblinks

Armstrong M (2008) *How To Be An Even Better Manager* (7th edn). London: Kogan Page.

CEC – *Guidelines for preparing a work plan* – https://tinyurl.com/6prmb87

Gravells A (2016) *Principles and Practices of Quality Assurance*. London: Learning Matters.

Mindtools – *Gantt charts* – https://tinyurl.com/y9jm5bg

Padlet – *Online notice board* – www.padlet.com

Wallace S and Gravells J (2007) *Leadership and Leading Teams*. Exeter: Learning Matters:

# 50 Writing self-assessment reports

| IQA activity | √ | EQA activity | √ | Deep dive activity | √ |
|---|---|---|---|---|---|
| In person | √ | Remote | √ | Electronic/online | √ |
| Includes learners | √ | Includes assessors | √ | Includes others | √ |
| Promotes standardisation | √ | Lead IQA role | √ | Quality improvement role | √ |

## What is it?

A self-assessment report (SAR) is an important management tool which looks back over the year, and captures the performance of an organisation. The person or people writing the SAR must consider, reflect and evaluate evidence of their organisation's performance, and make judgements about what went well and what needs to be done better or differently. This is produced in a format which maps the judgements against a set of pre-defined criteria. The SAR is concluded with an action plan known as a quality improvement plan (QIP) which details how strengths will be maintained and how any areas for improvement will be addressed over the coming year.

The criteria most commonly used for SAR writing are taken from the current Ofsted inspection handbook, in line with the Education Inspection Framework (EIF). The inspection handbooks have two parts. For example, in the *Further Education and Skills Inspection Handbook* (2020):

- Part 1 explains how further education and skills providers will be inspected.
- Part 2 is the evaluation schedule which contains the criteria most commonly used for writing a SAR.

The inspection handbooks contain the evaluation criteria inspectors use to judge the quality and standards of education, and the main types of evidence they use. There are separate handbooks for registered early years settings, maintained schools and academies, non-association independent schools and further education and skills providers in England.

The grading used in the evaluation schedule to make judgements is a four-point scale:

- grade 1 – outstanding
- grade 2 – good
- grade 3 – requires improvement
- grade 4 – inadequate.

Dividing your SAR into sections in line with the EIF, and the four key judgement areas as laid out in the evaluation schedule (see below), will support you to search thoroughly for information and evidence which enable you to demonstrate and evaluate the standard of education and care your learners receive.

The four key judgements are:

- quality of education (divided into three sections of intent, implementation and impact)
- behaviour and attitudes
- personal development
- leadership and management.

In addition, using the four key judgement areas in your SAR will enable you to grade the *overall effectiveness* of your provision which evaluates what it is like to be a learner at your organisation. If your provision is publicly funded, an overall grade should be given to each programme type offered, for example; education programmes for young people, apprenticeships, adults, or provision for learners with high needs.

Not all educational organisations are subject to inspection and regulation by Ofsted. For example, an organisation that is privately (not publicly) funded would not be in the scope for an inspection. However, the EIF and relevant inspection handbook would be a good framework for them to refer to, as it would give them a structure on which to base their self-assessment.

A SAR should also include evidence of feedback from staff, learner and employer question-naires, surveys and forums. It should take full account of how well safeguarding, equality and diversity practices are implemented and managed. It is also useful to involve another organisation as a *critical friend* to validate or moderate your judgements.

## What can it be used for?

Writing a factual and honest SAR is a powerful tool for reviewing and improving the quality of your provision. For large organisations, it is beneficial for every curriculum area to under-take a self-assessment review and develop a QIP which can feed into your organisation's overall SAR.

The QIP should address the main areas for improvement and include targeted timescales and measurable success criteria, and name the people who are responsible to ensure the actions are completed. It is useful to plan dates throughout the year to review and monitor the QIP to evaluate the progress being made.

# Resources

- SAR template with pre-defined criteria
- Ofsted's current inspection handbook
- Ofsted's current Education Inspection Framework (EIF)

# Advantages

👍 Helps to identify and rectify weaknesses in an organisation

👍 Can build awareness of risks and help to correct mistakes

👍 Can improve performance and help to maintain strengths

# Disadvantages

👎 Can be difficult to be objective when addressing the criteria

👎 Can be time-consuming to write

---

### Tip

Plan a staff development session to enable as many staff as possible to attend, and include them when creating the SAR. You could divide staff into four groups. Each group could discuss for 30 to 60 minutes one of the four key judgement areas from the evaluation schedule, and add their own comments and suggestions. They can then rotate to the next key area.

Ofsted often update their inspection handbook and EIF, so always check for the latest version which might include changes affecting the content of this chapter.

---

# Further reading and weblinks

Education and Training Foundation – *Excellence Gateway* – https://tinyurl.com/rxd3gzh

Education and Training Foundation – *SAR Guide Evaluative Words* – https://tinyurl.com/wjoqozf

Education Inspection Framework (EIF) (2019) – https://tinyurl.com/y2endkyw

*Further Education and Skills Inspection Handbook* (2020) – https://tinyurl.com/y6es6aun

# Appendix 1

## Example of a completed IQA sample plan and tracking sheet

Qualification: Level 2 Customer Service
Assessor: P Jones

IQA: H Rahl

| Learner & location | Start date / Registration date & number | Unit 101 | Unit 102 | Unit 103 | Unit 104 | Unit 105 | Summative | End date / Certification date |
|---|---|---|---|---|---|---|---|---|
| Ann Bex X Company | 01 Nov 10 Nov 1234ITG | Jan Sampled on 12 Jan AR | Feb Sampled on 18 Feb X AR | Aug | Sept | Nov | Dec | |
| Eve Holler X Company | 01 Nov 10 Nov 1235ITG | Jan Sampled on 12 Jan √ | Mar Sampled on 18 Mar X AR | | | | | |
| Terri Frame Y Company | 04 Jan 14 Jan 7854URE | April Sampled on 13 April | | June | | | | |
| Jon Vanquis Z Company | 04 Jan 14 Jan 7855URE | May | | | Aug | | | |
| Naomi Black Z Company | 04 Jan 14 Jan 7856URE | July | | | | Sept | | |
| Xuxia Chi 123 Company | 12 Aug 24 Aug 9193IUR | | | | | | Oct | |
| Key: | AR – action required | | X – problems noticed in this unit | | | √ – no problems noticed in this unit | | |

*To future-proof this book years have not been added to dates, however they should be added when you complete any records.*

# Appendix 2

**Example of a completed standardisation record for assessed work**

| Learner: Ann Bex | | | Original assessor: P Jones |
|---|---|---|---|
| Qualification/unit: Level 2 Customer Service | | | Standardising assessor: M Singh |
| Aspect/s standardised: Unit 101 evidence and assessment records | | | Date: 12 February |

| Checklist | Yes | No | Comments | Recommended action points |
|---|---|---|---|---|
| Is there an agreed assessment plan with SMART targets? (specific, measureable, achievable, relevant, time bound) | Y | | Your plan had very clear SMART targets with realistic dates for achievement. | |
| Are the assessment methods appropriate and sufficient? Which methods were used? | Y | | Appropriate and sufficient methods were used. Methods used: observation, questioning, products and witness testimonies. | |
| Does the evidence meet ALL the required criteria? | Y | | All assessment criteria have been met though the various assessment methods. | |
| Does the evidence meet VARCS? (valid, authentic, reliable, current, sufficient) | Y | | You have ensured all the VARCS points. You also took into consideration an aspect you hadn't planned to assess, but that naturally occurred during an observation. | |
| Is there a feedback record clearly showing what has been achieved? Is it adequate and developmental? | | N | Your feedback confirms your learner's achievements but is not developmental. | When providing feedback, you should be more developmental with your comments to stretch and challenge your learner. |

| | | | |
|---|---|---|---|
| Has subsequent action been identified? (If applicable) | N | The feedback record showed what had been achieved, however no further action had been identified for your learner to aim towards. | You should plan which units will be assessed next, and set target dates for their achievement. |
| Do you agree with the assessment decision? | Y | I agree with the decision you made, however I do feel you could have reduced the number of workplace observations. | |
| Are all relevant documents signed and dated? (Including countersignatures if applicable) | N | As you are still working towards your assessor award, you need to ensure your decisions have been checked and countersigned by a qualified assessor. | Obtain countersignatures. |
| Are original assessment records stored separately from the learner's work? | N | You have given your original records to your learner. The original must be kept secure for three years in the assessor office. | You need to ensure you keep the originals of all records and give your learner the copies. |

General comments:

Although there are a few 'Nos' in the checklist, this does not affect my judgement as I agree with your decision for this learner.

All your records are in place, however don't forget to keep originals in the office and give your learner a copy. This is part of our organisation's policy due to some learners having amended the original in their favour. It's harder to amend a copy as the pen colour is more prominent. However, we will be moving to electronic records shortly so this will change.

Comments from original assessor in response to the above:

*I agree with your feedback, I had forgotten about keeping original records and only giving a photocopy to my learner. I will ensure I do this in future. I wasn't able to get hold of my countersignatory as he was on holiday, I will make sure he reads my records and signs them upon his return. I will then take a copy ready to use as evidence for my assessor award. I realise that I must give more developmental feedback and agree future targets when I am with my learner.*

*To future-proof this book a year has not been added to the date, however it should be added when you complete any records.*

# Appendix 3

**Example of a completed work plan for a lead internal quality assurer**

| IQA name: | H Rahl | | | | | | | | | | | | |
|---|---|---|---|---|---|---|---|---|---|---|---|---|---|
| **Objective:** | To plan, monitor and review the IQA process in accordance with organisational requirements (Customer Service qualifications) | | | | | | | | | | | | |
| **Activities & month:** | **Jan** | **Feb** | **Mar** | **Apr** | **May** | **Jun** | **Jul** | **Aug** | **Sep** | **Oct** | **Nov** | **Dec** | **Notes** |
| Produce IQA sampling plan for self, ensure other IQAs complete theirs | 5th | | | | | | | | | | | | |
| Produce IQA observation plan, ensure other IQAs complete theirs | 5th | | | | | | | | | | | | |
| Plan team meeting dates and delegate the role of the chair on a rota basis | 12th | | | | | | | | | | | | |
| Plan standardisation activities and dates | | 1st | | | | | | | | | | | |
| Prepare for external quality assurance visit | | | | | | | | | | | | | Inform all staff and hold an additional meeting before and after the visit |

| Task | Notes |
|---|---|
| Meet with external quality assurer | Reserve a room beforehand |
| Review assessment/IQA policies and procedures, including IQA rationale and individual strategies | Ask for feedback from relevant staff beforehand |
| Review assessment and IQA documentation | " |
| Review and update IQA activities | " |
| Carry out staff appraisals | |
| Produce report and statistics regarding appeals and complaints | Could be done in December if necessary |
| Write annual IQA report for directors | Distribute two weeks beforehand |
| Attend annual directors' meeting | |

*To future-proof this book years have not been added to the months, however they should be added when you complete any records.*

# Appendix 4

## Career guidance for schools and colleges

## The matrix Standard

*The matrix standard is a framework for organisations to assess and measure their information, advice and guidance services. It aims to support individuals in their choice of career, learning, work and life goals.* (https://tinyurl.com/y2csmsrp)

In England, the Department for Education (DfE) supports the matrix Standard as the quality framework for accrediting information, advice and guidance (IAG) services for contracts including the National Careers Service, its subcontractors and other services delivered under the Educations Skills Funding Agency (ESFA).

The matrix Standard supports organisations to improve their services by benchmarking them against best practice. Accreditation is offered to organisations who meet the full standard. Accreditation is an outcome-based independent assessment that looks not only at processes used to support IAG, but also other results such as learner and staff feedback, retention, pass rates and learner destinations. Once achieved it is monitored annually and reassessed every three years.

## The Gatsby benchmarks

Gatsby is a charitable foundation which acts as a facilitator for projects, designing, developing, overseeing, and sometimes delivering activities. In 2013 Gatsby commissioned Sir John Holman to research what could be done to improve career guidance in England's education system. After completing the research, *The Good Career Guidance Report* was produced which identified a set of eight benchmarks that schools can use as a framework for improving their careers provision.

The eight Gatsby benchmarks of *Good Career Guidance* for schools are:

1.   A stable careers programme

2.   Learning from career and labour market information

3.   Addressing the needs of each pupil

4.   Linking curriculum learning to careers

5.   Encounters with employers and employees

6.   Experiences of workplaces

7.   Encounters with further and higher education

8.   Personal guidance

Following the success of the Gatsby benchmarks for schools, a consultation was undertaken with further education colleges and the *Good Career Guidance: Benchmarks for colleges* was created.

The Gatsby benchmarks for schools and colleges are designed to inspire learners towards further study and to enable them to make informed decisions whenever choices are open to them.

# Further reading and weblinks

Education & Skills Funding Agency – https://tinyurl.com/mdrltn8

Gatsby – *Good Career Guidance* – https://tinyurl.com/tvs7kpa

Good Career Guidance (Benchmarks for Colleges leaflet) –https://tinyurl.com/y9ya847p

Good Career Guidance (Benchmarks for Schools leaflet) – https://tinyurl.com/ya9l73ht

Matrix Standard – *Evaluation* – https://tinyurl.com/y2csmsrp

The matrix Standard – *What is the matrix Standard?* – https://tinyurl.com/y9d2zqvt

# Index